Praise for World War II Indiana Landmarks

For several years, Ronald May has done truly exemplary, valuable work in capturing World War II history involving Indiana. His interviews with scores of Hoosier veterans are a trove, particularly because so many of his interview subjects have passed away and are no longer able to share their experiences. In addition to his talents as an interviewer and as a writer, Ron does tremendous research as a World War II historian. This enables him to share insights and add context and depth to his work.

—*Nelson Price, author of* Indiana Legends *and host of* Hoosier History Live *on WICR-FM*

Ron May captures the reader's interest in this historical journey across the Indiana landscape to explore the sites related to World War II. He brings the project to life with his descriptive gifts. While foremost a journey about historical places, it is the human stories he uses to sustain the reader's interest. Intended or not, he also activates strong feelings about America's patriotism and leaves the reader torn between the pride we have for the Greatest Generation and today's nation of division. It also triggers memories of our own family members who served and prompts reviews of old family albums and letters. His book will prompt readers to plan trips to see these marvels of history and the stories that touch our hearts.

—*Richard D. Chegar, Major General, U.S. Army (Ret.)*

WORLD WAR II
INDIANA
LANDMARKS

RONALD P. MAY

THE
History
PRESS

Published by The History Press
Charleston, SC
www.historypress.com

Cover images taken by author.

First published 2023

Manufactured in the United States

ISBN 9781467154116

Library of Congress Control Number: 2022950087

CONTENTS

ACKNOWLEDGEMENTS

The foundation for my part of my book was laid long ago by the Indiana War History Commission and its book, *The Hoosier Training Ground*, published in 1952 and edited by Dorothy Riker. It was only seven years after the war's conclusion, but the commission was forward-thinking enough to realize the treasure it could offer future generations by researching and writing about the building of army and navy installations, airfields and training centers in Indiana during the early 1940s. The volume is a masterpiece of Indiana military history during World War II.

I am indebted to the many people who assisted me with my research. Some I met personally, several I spoke to on the phone and others were known to me only through e-mail correspondence. They were all tremendous blessings. I couldn't have written the book without their help. At the risk of forgetting some people, I especially would like to thank the following:

Naval Air Station Bunker Hill: Thomas R. Jennings, the executive director of the Grissom Air Museum, who opened his office to me for the day and aided in gathering history and personal stories; Beverly Parker and her staff of the Miami County Historical Society in Peru, who allowed me to share their office space as I examined boxes of photos from their archives; and Maureen (Rene) Williams and her husband, Michael, who opened their home to me and my wife and shared invaluable information about her father's service as a flight instructor at Naval Air Station Bunker Hill.

ALLEN COUNTY WAR MEMORIAL COLISEUM: Nathan J. Dennison, vice-president of sales at the Allen County War Memorial Coliseum. He personally gave me a tour of the Veterans Memorial Hall inside the coliseum, provided helpful background information and supplied me with some historic and current photos.

VETERANS NATIONAL MEMORIAL SHRINE AND MUSEUM: Robert Thomas, curator of the museum, who personally opened locked displays and told me about the collection of items from World War II.

KINGSBURY ORDNANCE PLANT: Bruce Johnson, historian at the La Porte County Historical Society Museum, who pulled all the information on the Kingsbury Ordnance Plant from its archives for my review; and Jacey Dare, collections manager, for the same, as well as assisting me in acquiring photos and permission.

AVON WORLD WAR II MEMORIAL PARK: Larry Wright, son of General Clyde (Chet) Wright, for helping me secure photographs and sharing information about his father; and William (Bill) Wolfe, sculptor of the statue used in the Avon World War II Memorial Park, for sharing photos and memories of his time interacting with General Wright.

ATTERBURY-BAKALAR MUSEUM: David Day, historian at the museum, who gave me a personal tour, provided information on select exhibits of interest and sent me digital information on the museum; Nick Firestone, president of the museum for his helpful correspondence with me; and Rhonda Bolner, who helped me acquire some period photos of Atterbury Army Air Field and personnel.

ERNIE PYLE MUSEUM: Steve Key, president of the Friends of Ernie Pyle Board of Directors, who sent me photos of Pyle and provided some helpful editing suggestions on my writeup of the museum.

CAMP ATTERBURY: Jim Goen, community relations for Camp Atterbury's Welcome Center, and Chief Warrant Officer (Ret.) Myles Clayburn, both of whom assisted me with finding photos for the Camp Atterbury chapter.

WORLD WAR II MEMORIAL INDY: John Bellinger and the William Rudy family for sharing the story of Rudy's service and providing photos.

CANDLES Holocaust Museum: Trent Andrews, facilities and operations coordinator at CANDLES, who searched for and sent me several photos of Eva Kor.

Veterans Memorial Museum of Terre Haute: Brian Mundell, owner and curator of the museum, who opened the museum for me during off hours, gave me a personal tour and offered background on several feature World War II exhibits.

Charlestown Public Library: Staff who assisted me in finding the archives for the Indiana Army Ammunition Plant.

Navy Ammunition Depot Crane: Jeff Naga, public affairs officer at Naval Support Activity Crane, who arranged for my on-site tour of the base and provided some referrals for my research; Pamela Ingram, public affairs officer for Naval Surface Warfare Center, Crane Division, who spent the day with me as my official escort and drove me to sites for taking photos; Ben Embry, cultural resource manager at Crane, for giving me an overview of the base history and providing me with a digital photo presentation; and Rick Bowling, director of the Martin County Historical Society in Shoals, for providing information about Crane during a tour of the museum and helping me access some Martin County oral history documents related to the Navy Ammunition Depot.

Indiana Military Museum: Mark Kratzner, curator of the Red Skelton Museum of American Comedy in Vincennes, for sending me information of Skelton's service in the military as well as photos of him in uniform.

Jefferson Proving Ground: Ron Roaks, vice-president of the board of directors for the Jefferson County Historical Society History Center in Madison, who assisted me with finding vintage photos of the Jefferson Proving Ground; and Mike Moore, former employee at JPG, who offered information on the history of JPG and some people who worked there during World War II.

Freeman Army Airfield Museum: Larry Bothe, curator of the museum, who assisted me in finding personal stories and photographs of several cadets who trained at Freeman Army Airfield.

I also wish to thank the following for their assistance and support for the entire project:

Dave McCoy, who created the map of Indiana and inserted the chapter numbers in their respective locations.

Major General Richard D. Chegar, U.S. Army (Ret.), for reading an advance copy of the book and offering his endorsement.

Larry Cracraft, my proofreader. The son-in-law of a World War II veteran, Ronald Lux, whose story appears in the third volume of my book series, Larry graciously approached me to offer his services as a proofreader for this project. He caught many errors in my early drafts and made helpful grammatical suggestions that always improved clarity.

The History Press and John Rodrigue, who accepted my book proposal and made the publishing process clear, smooth and seamless.

My wife, Glenda, for enduring the seven months that I spent writing this book. She did the lion's share of taking care of everything at home so that I could devote myself to completing this project. I couldn't have done it without you, sweetheart. You have my undying love and appreciation.

And finally, a heartfelt thanks for the men and women of Indiana who answered the call to service when our nation went to war. Their ingenuity and efforts inflated the significance of Indiana much larger than its actual borders. What they accomplished is an inspiration. I'm proud to stand in their shadows and do what I can to pass the torch of their Hoosier Spirit to the next generation.

INTRODUCTION

On November 21, 1941, the hull of the newest *South Dakota*–class battleship was launched at the Newport News Shipbuilding and Dry Dock Company at Newport News, Virginia. Margaret Robbins, the daughter of then Indiana governor Henry F. Schricker, was on hand to christen the ship the USS *Indiana* (BB-58).[1] Sixteen days later, on December 7, Japanese forces attacked Pearl Harbor, and Indiana—the ship and the state—was suddenly destined for war.

Commissioned in April 1942, the ship bearing Indiana's name saw extensive action in the South and Central Pacific campaigns, including the invasions of the Gilbert and Marshall Islands and the Battle of the Philippine Sea. In the war's final months, it participated in the invasions at Iwo Jima and Okinawa, where it shot down several kamikazes. Its final combat action came as it fired its sixteen-inch guns on mainland Japan in the last weeks of the war. Following the war's conclusion, the *Indiana* was placed in the Navy's Reserve Fleet until 1947, when it was removed from the Naval Vessel Register.[2]

You won't find the USS *Indiana* today, at least not intact. It was sold for scrap in 1963.[3] But you can find parts of the historic ship and its spirit scattered across the Hoosier landscape from as far north as South Bend to the southernmost tip of Evansville and as far west as Terre Haute to the northeastern city of Fort Wayne.

An inventory of the known parts and artifacts from the battleship and their current homes includes the following:[4]

- A bronze crucifix used on the *Indiana* for Roman Catholic services was donated to Notre Dame University after it was decommissioned in 1962.
- One of the ship's massive anchors stands proudly at the Veterans Plaza of the Allen County War Memorial in Fort Wayne.
- Part of the ship's teakwood deck was used to make the top of the governor's desk and can be viewed while on a tour of the governor's office in the Indiana State Capitol building.
- The ship's battle flag and two of its bells are displayed at the Indiana War Memorial Museum in Indianapolis.
- The ship's main bell has found a home at the former Heslar Naval Armory (today Riverside High School) in Indianapolis.
- The ship's wheel is displayed in Shortridge High School, also in Indianapolis.
- The largest parts of the ship's remains—its prow (the tip of the bow), mast and some of its gun mounts—are standing proudly in front of Memorial Stadium at West Gate 3 on the campus of Indiana University in Bloomington.[5]
- A sister university to the west, Indiana State University in Terre Haute, received the *Indiana*'s signal flags.
- A Jewish prayer shawl, used in the ship's Jewish worship services, is in a collection at the Evansville Museum of Art and Science.

This wide dispersal of the former battleship's parts throughout the Hoosier state is a fitting metaphor for the contributions of the many scattered people, cities and towns in Indiana during World War II. Factories in Gary produced the steel used in making tanks, planes and jeeps. Ordnance plants rose from the fertile farm soil, taking the place of Indiana's ubiquitous cornfields near Kingsbury, Terre Haute and Charlestown. Public and private universities throughout the state offered specialized military training programs to prepare service members for specific ratings. And new military bases were quickly built in Fort Wayne, Bunker Hill, Edinburgh, Columbus, Crane and Seymour, training thousands of men, and a great many women, for war service.

In the years following the conclusion of the war, memorials of limestone and granite bearing the names of the heroic dead began dotting the state. They still pay tribute to the 11,680 Hoosiers who died during the war.[6] Museums—some in large cities and others in small towns—have been built

USS *Indiana. U.S. Navy.*

in more recent decades to retell Indiana's war service and preserve the memories of those who participated in World War II and other wars.

All these are pieces of the great Indiana wartime puzzle or, better yet, symbolic parts of the great *Indiana* ship that represented the state. As much as I'd love to find and include every piece of Indiana's World War II story, it is beyond the scope of one book to do so.[7] It is easier to look at the stars in the sky and imagine the many ways that Hoosiers contributed to the war than for me to attempt a complete written inventory of every base, every company, every product and every person's specific role. What I have attempted to do in this book is feature select bases, memorials, monuments and museums that can help us remember the broad Hoosier involvement in the war. These are places that can still be seen and visited today.

This book's chapters are divided into the three geographical regions of Indiana: North, Central and South. A key next to the state map identifies the approximate physical location for each chapter subject.

Included in each chapter is a personal story of an Indiana citizen or military member who was connected in some way to the place I have

Indiana University Memorial Stadium with USS *Indiana* prow and gun displayed. *ZCash1104, Creative Commons Attribution-Share Alike 4.0 International.*

USS *Indiana* anchor at Allen County War Memorial, Fort Wayne. *Ronald May.*

featured in that chapter. Some of these individuals were personally interviewed by me, and fuller accounts of their stories can be found in their respective chapter in my three-volume book series, *Our Service Our Stories*. Other personal stories come from oral interview archives, newspaper articles or family members of the deceased. It was my conviction from the beginning of this project that the best way to tell the story of each place was to have a personal story reveal some of the spirit and significance of the place. Indeed, without people's stories, the meaning of places is greatly diminished.

Some of the chapters in this book are expanded revisions of articles I wrote for the *Martinsville Reporter-Times* newspaper from 2012 to 2018 in a feature series on Indiana sites and World War II. Chapters that include revisions of these articles are noted by a footnote at the end of the chapter.

It is my hope that this book will show how much the state of Indiana was involved in the war effort during World War II. I encourage readers to visit these historic landmarks and reflect on the Hoosier efforts and ingenuity of men and women who served as military members, civilian laborers or supportive families in a time of global conflict. As we take the time to gratefully remember their contributions, we celebrate and affirm our Hoosier heritage.

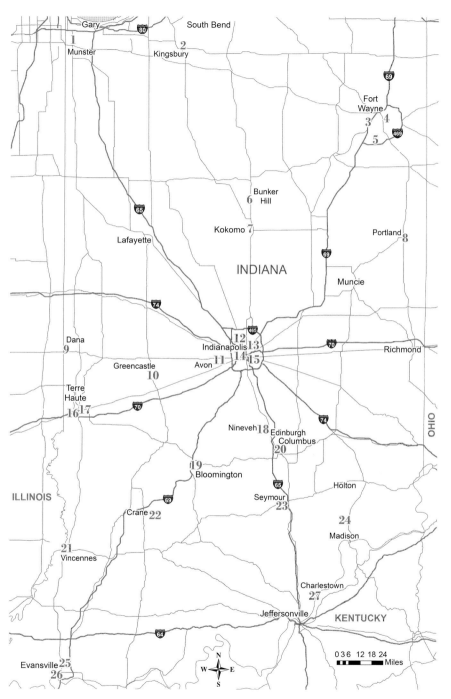

Indiana map with chapter sites. *Created by and courtesy of Dave McCoy.*

PART I

NORTHERN INDIANA

1

COMMUNITY VETERANS MEMORIAL

The Community Veterans Memorial in Munster is an expansive nine-acre park in Northwest Indiana that commemorates U.S. involvement in the major wars of the twentieth century. Located at 9710 Calumet Avenue, on the west side of the road, half a mile east of the Illinois border, the memorial is a major attraction in the region.

While other war memorials often consist of stone markers listing names of those who served and summaries of war narratives, the Community Veterans Memorial does far more. It effectively conveys the tragedy and horror of combat with each of its war displays.

Visiting the memorial is an immersive and visceral experience. Visitors see and even feel the horror of combat as they gaze at the contorted faces and bodies of those depicted in life-size bronze statues and view the laser-etched images in granite. Physical objects, approximating the actual terrain of combat settings, are integrated in each of the memorials and add to the angst already produced by the statues. Metal beams, massive concrete slabs, war memorabilia, varied topography and unique landscape features (including plantings of the species of trees and plants from the different countries) all combine to transport the visitor to the scene of battle through which they can consider its true cost in human lives.[8]

The day I visited, black smoke rose behind the memorial as a Boy Scout troop burned worn and discarded U.S. flags. The dark smoke, combined with the gray, low-hanging clouds, provided a somber and ominous canopy over an already sobering memorial park.

The Pacific War Monument. A marine reaches toward the hand of an airman trapped after his plane crashes. *Ronald May.*

Moving past the flagpoles at the park's entrance, visitors encounter the history trail timeline composed of individual bricks that wrap around the park's walkway, identifying key dates and events that led up to each war. A tower kiosk with prerecorded audio narration summarizes the war narrative at each respective commemorative site.

After passing the World War I memorial, the visitor is confronted by the tail of a P-51 fighter plane tilted down and embedded into the concrete outcropping to convey a crash. The slab features a granite face that reveals laser etchings of photographic scenes from the Pacific war, including the attack on Pearl Harbor, the sinking of the USS *Lexington* in the Coral Sea, the damaged USS *Yorktown*, U.S. dive bombers in action at Midway, the battle at the base of Mount Suribachi on Iwo Jima and the deadly suicide missions of the Japanese kamikazes.[9]

A lone marine in full combat gear kneels at the base of the triangular slab. His arm is reaching out with concern and compassion toward a single hand, presumably of the downed pilot, protruding from a crack in the slab. It is a moving scene of destruction and sacrifice.

Just beyond this display is the memorial commemorating the war in Europe. Here the visitor sees the horrified face of an army radioman who has just landed on Omaha Beach. He is kneeling beside one of the steel beach obstacles the Germans placed across the shoreline to hinder the Allied landings. The radioman is shouting out an order or calling out in urgency for

The European War Monument. A bronze radioman calling for comrades on Omaha Beach. *Ronald May*.

assistance. He holds his rifle in his left hand—it is pointed inland toward the enemy. His right arm is extended outward. In grotesque fashion, a mutilated arm seems to drop from under his top arm, suggesting some horrific damage to his appendage.[10]

Behind the soldier are items that have fallen to the shore in the aftermath of the landing's carnage: a hand rising from the sand and grasping a canteen, a pair of combat boots, a dagger, a grenade and an ammo pouch beside two canteens.

The back side of the triangular slab has a granite face that shows laser-etched photographic scenes from the European theater of conflict: the landing at Omaha Beach, fighting on Mount Cassino in Italy, the flight of a B-24 Liberator, a wintry Bastogne under siege in the Belgium Ardennes and disturbing Holocaust scenes from concentration camps.[11]

Off to the side of the European war memorial is the Homefront Monument. A tan-colored cement structure curves toward the European and Pacific memorials. The structure is the artistic shape of a mother's arms, a Great Mother archetype, reaching out toward her sons and daughters caught in the overseas combat. In the center of the cement structure is a large bronze plate of a woman dressed in factory clothes and wearing a bandana. She symbolizes the more than 6 million women who worked in factories and mills producing the necessary war products.[12] She faces a circular opening in

Homefront Monument. A "Rosie" looks out through the portal to the city where she works to support the war effort. *Ronald May.*

the concrete structure and looks out toward the steel mill cities beyond that once produced the essential material for war.[13] In her sightline are the large flagpoles flying the national ensign and the service flags of the armed forces at the park's entrance.

Around the woman are bronze handwritten letters and excerpts etched in granite that pay tribute to women's losses and contributions in the war effort. Two excerpts are especially impactful:

> *"I'm war. Remember me? 'Yes, you're asleep,' you say, 'and you kill men.' Look in my game-bag, fuller than you think. I kill marriages...I kill families...I drink gold...I am the game that nobody can win. What's yours is mine, what's mine is still my own. I'm war. Remember me."* (Mary Hacker)

> *"If you can drive a car, you can run a machine." "I flunked in charm and social composure, but I passed in welding and riveting." (Rosie the Riveter, cartoon from Lockheed Aircraft)*

World War II veteran Ray McDonald, a native of nearby Gary, Indiana, missed the carnage of combat depicted in these World War II memorials. But he did not avoid the war. His early life and subsequent military service matched the bookends of U.S. involvement in the war.

Ray McDonald at home in Gary.
Ray McDonald.

Born on July 6, 1927, he was fourteen years old when Japan attacked Pearl Harbor. Coming of age during the U.S. entrance into the war, he participated in scrap metal salvage drives with his Boy Scout troop, trained in ROTC and followed the war's progress while attending high school.[14]

On October 15, 1945, he traveled to Camp Atterbury, Indiana, for processing into the U.S. Army. While there, he accepted an opportunity to join the U.S. Army Air Forces. When it was discovered that he knew how to type, he was sent to clerk typist school at SAC Field (Strategic Air Command) in San Antonio, Texas.[15]

In July 1946, McDonald left to serve with the U.S. occupation forces in Japan. He was stationed at Chitose Army Air Base on Hokkaido Island, home to the 49th Fighter Squadron, 5th Air Force. "It was good duty," he recalled. "I worked in the headquarters building in the officers classification, maintaining officers' records."[16] While there, McDonald witnessed Japanese citizens of a defeated imperial nation attempting to recover and rebuild following the end of a cataclysmic war. He served in Japan from August 1946 to April 1947.

The idea for the Community Veterans Memorial came fifty years after McDonald's war service, as area veterans began talking about the need for a memorial to honor America's war heroes. Planning for the memorial began in 1999 with a threefold goal of remembering, educating and challenging people about U.S. involvement in wars.[17]

Community Veterans Memorial was dedicated on June 1, 2003.[18] The land for the park had been donated in 2000 by Community Hospital of Munster, located 1.5 miles north of the park. The memorial cost more than $3.2 million to build. The Community Foundation of Northwest Indiana funded $3 million of the project, and the rest was raised by donations.[19]

The Community Veterans Memorial was rededicated in 2007 as the Edward P. Robinson Community Veterans Memorial. Robinson served as the first administrator of Community Hospital in Munster for more than thirty-six years. An air force veteran who served in the Korean Conflict with the 5th Air Force—ironically the same air force division that McDonald had served in during World War II—he worked tirelessly to bring the Community Veterans Memorial to fruition.[20]

Renowned sculptors Omri Amrany and his wife, Julie Rotblatt-Amrany, created each of the Community Veterans Memorial centerpieces.[21] Born in Israel, Amrany served with the Israeli Defense Forces as a paratrooper during the Yom Kippur War in 1973 and witnessed the deaths of fellow soldiers. He used his art to therapeutically work through his own grief over combat and loss. Amrany moved to the United States and became a naturalized citizen. He and Julie opened the Fine Art Studio in Fort Sheridan, Illinois, in 1992.[22] "We hoped to create a park for reflection and contemplation," Rotblatt-Amrany said at the opening of the memorial. "The different vignettes show war decade after decade. People will be faced with powerful visual images that will leave them feeling uncomfortable and tragic. Those are the realities of war."[23]

Such "realities of war" are impossible to miss while visiting the Community Veterans Memorial. But it is equally hard, especially with the waving U.S. flag at the memorial's entrance, to miss the reality of the freedom secured for our nation through these sacrifices.

2

KINGSBURY ORDNANCE PLANT

Northern Indiana is known for its flat topography and fertile soil. In 1940, it became known for something else as the U.S. government converted twenty square miles of that farmland into a large ordnance production plant.[24]

Kingsbury, Indiana, was a small dot on the map in northwestern Indiana. Located seven miles south of the city of LaPorte in LaPorte County, the area was dominated by farms. By 1937, the U.S. Ordnance Department was considering the area as a possible site for a large ordnance plant.[25] The area was highly desirable due to its low population density, inland location far away from the danger of coastal bombing by Germany, access to roads and railways, ample water supply and proximity to larger towns for a potential labor force.[26] In 1940, the decision was made to acquire thirteen thousand acres and build the Kingsbury Ordnance Plant (KOP).[27]

The shell-loading plant, one of the largest in the country, was built by the Todd and Brown Construction Company between 1940 and 1941 at an initial cost of $47 million.[28]

The transformation of the topography was immense: 80 miles of new road were built on the thirteen thousand acres of farm fields.[29] When the plant was completed, its infrastructure included 80 miles of train track and 134 miles of roads.[30] According to the Michigan City, Indiana Public Library's February 15, 2018 Facebook post, by the time the plant was completed, there were more than one thousand structures.

The Honorable William T. Schulte of Indiana praised the partnership between the army engineers and civilian supervisors of the Todd and Brown Construction Company. He noted in his June 5, 1941 remarks to the U.S. House of Representatives the scale of the project, as well as the anticipated output:

> *As originally planned, the daily output of this plant is to be 40,000 fixed rounds of 20 mm.; 50,000 fixed rounds of 37 mm.; 40,000 fixed rounds of 75 mm., or 90 mm., or 105 mm.; 40,000 fixed rounds of 60 mm. trench mortar, with corresponding fuzes and boosters for the above. One-hundred-and thirty-five storage buildings had to be constructed with the following operating buildings: Five load lines, two fuze lines, two booster lines, one ammonia nitrate amatol plant, administration buildings and shops, fire department buildings and equipment staff, mess halls, hospitals, guards' quarters, and so forth.*[31]

The primary mission of KOP was "to load shells of different caliber, assemble fuzes, boosters, detonators and primers, and pack complete rounds of ammunition, in ever-increasing quantities for shipment overseas."[32] Shells were made for projectiles from 20mm up to 105mm.

Fuze line assembly building, Kingsbury Ordnance Plant. *LaPorte County Historical Society and Museum.*

On October 13, 1941, KOP produced its first shell for delivery, a 60mm projectile.[33] The attack on Pearl Harbor came less than two months later, confirming the wisdom of the U.S. government's decision to build the plant.

The population of workers at KOP grew steadily. There were 5,000 workers in December 1941, and five months later, in May 1942, the number of workers peaked at 20,785.[34]

The work was difficult and dangerous, especially on the assembly lines, and required winning the battle of concentration over fatigue. "Kingsbury's automated assembly line forced workers to remain alert and productive despite tasks that might be physically taxing, repetitive, or both; the assembly lines were only dimly lit, and many of the materials had to be quickly assembled with tweezers. All workers had to wear protective clothing and shower before leaving, as one chemical component turned any exposed hair or skin orange."[35]

Housing shortages for the growing number of workers were addressed in the fall of 1942 by building a new town called Kingsford Heights, which offered 2,600 affordable homes for the influx of employees. Dormitories for single people were also built. Local homeowners also rented rooms to those who needed them.[36] The whole area of Kingsbury, Indiana, was transformed into a beehive of workers and dwellers.

In 1943, recruitment efforts for new workers extended well beyond Indiana's boundaries. People from as far as Pennsylvania to the east, Minnesota to the north, Colorado to the west and the Gulf states to the south were recruited to work at KOP.[37] Right from the start, women made up a significant portion of the workforce. Initially, one third of the workers were women, but with the increasing number of male workers called into military service, women represented 45 percent of the workforce by the war's end.[38]

Naoma Zellers was one of those women. The Kewana, Indiana native began work at Kingsbury Ordnance Plant in the fall of 1941. She had just graduated from high school.[39] "One of my girlfriends said, 'Let's go up and apply for jobs.' So, we did," recalled Naoma in an interview with the author. "We didn't think we would get the jobs, but we did." Both girls traveled the forty-eight miles to Kingsbury each day in a carpool.[40]

"My first job was putting black pellets in primer things as they came by," Naoma remembered. "I also later weighed primers to see if they had the right amount of TNT in them. Then I became an inspector. I inspected these great big vats which held melted TNT. I took the temperature of the melting TNT. If the temperature wasn't right, I had to stir it."[41]

Naoma (Zellers) Seidel, age seventeen. *Naoma Seidel.*

There were risks while working with the explosives. "We wore safety clothes and shoes as well as white coveralls," recalled Naoma. "We were warned about the danger, but we were too young to be scared."[42]

The plant, which included underground bomb shelters, was designed to protect its workers from accidents. So too were the presence of government inspectors. "Everything was very particular there," Naoma said. "There was a U.S. inspector on site watching what was going on so things were done right, and no one would steal things."[43]

KOP progressively became a diverse workforce. In April 1942, the plant began to accept African Americans into its labor force.[44] "I had never been around a black person while growing up," Naoma recalled. "Some were at the plant working as bathroom attendants and cleaning ladies."[45] People of color weren't just on janitorial crews. As the need for workers grew, so did their opportunity to step into a variety of other positions. Some African Americans were assigned the most dangerous jobs.[46]

Naoma worked at KOP from the fall of 1941 to 1944. "I felt like I accomplished something," she said, looking back at her wartime employment.[47] Indeed, she and the others accomplished a great deal. Throughout its operation during World War II, the plant produced massive amounts of ordnance. A typical day of production included "180,000 point-detonating fuzes, 46,671 40 mm. high explosives shells (MK 11); 500,000 complete rounds of 20 mm. ammunition, and more than a score of other items."[48]

In recognition for its outstanding work, the Kingsbury Ordnance Plant received the Army-Navy "E" Award for Production Excellence in January 1943. During the forty-six months of operation from October 13, 1941, through August 14, 1945, the KOP produced 285,369,803 units of ordnance.[49]

Following the conclusion of World War II, the plant was closed. It was used again briefly during the Korean War. All production ended on March 31, 1959, and the government sold the property.[50]

Today, the Kingsbury State Fish and Wildlife Area occupies part of the former KOP. An industrial park with various companies fills a good portion

Kingsbury Ordnance Plant Buildings, used today by Kingsbury Industrial Park. *Ronald May.*

of the rest of the land. Some of those businesses are still using original buildings from the KOP. Other buildings are vacant and slowly becoming ruins as nature reclaims its ground.

You can still see much of what used to be the Kingsbury Ordnance Plant by driving east along Hupp Road, which is accessed just north of the State Highway 35 and State Highway 6 intersection, a few miles south of the city of LaPorte. The area remains a visible testimony to Northern Indiana's significant contribution to the war effort.

3

VETERANS NATIONAL MEMORIAL SHRINE AND MUSEUM

The Veterans National Memorial Shrine and Museum had its origin on the battlefield of northeastern France in World War I. In July 1918, during the heat of combat at the Second Battle of Marne, Eric Scott was serving with the 3rd Infantry Division, 6th Combat Engineers. Seeing the carnage of wounded and dead comrades around him and facing his own mortality, the Fort Wayne native made a promise to God that if he survived the war, "no veteran will ever be forgotten."[51]

Scott kept his promise and then some. In 1945, he and his wife, Cleo, purchased forty acres and a farmhouse seven miles west of Fort Wayne at the corner of Yellow River and O'Day Roads. Their goal was to create a veterans museum on the property. After their farmhouse burned down in 1948, the Scotts built a new home out of stone and brick and stored war memorabilia in some of the new space they designated for their museum. They officially opened the National War Veterans of American History Inc. in 1951.[52] One year later, the couple began hosting reunions for the surviving men from Scott's 6th Combat Engineers Army unit. The men contributed some of their own memorabilia for the museum, and the collection grew. In the 1970s, the Scotts built a memorial chapel on their property. A twenty-five-bell carillon was installed that played military and patriotic tunes for the next twenty years.[53]

Prior to Scott's death on April 13, 1981, he and his wife deeded the property to the museum's board of directors so that his mission to remember veterans would continue for future generations.[54] That long-range dream

Submarine torpedo, Veterans National Memorial Shrine and Museum. *Ronald May*.

almost came to an end. In the decades after Scott's death, veterans' groups from different war eras installed memorials on the property, but the museum's board of directors struggled to keep the museum open. Finances dwindled, and by 2017, the county was about to foreclose on the property. Fortunately, in 2018, a donor stepped forward and paid the delinquent bills, keeping Scott's legacy and promise alive.

In the meantime, the National Military History Center and Victory Museum in Auburn, Indiana, which had opened in 2003, closed its doors after operating for fifteen years. Some of the volunteers from that museum formed a new nonprofit called Veterans National Memorial Shrine and Museum, elected a board of directors and took over the operations of the defunct National War Veterans of American History Inc. started by Scott.[55]

Today, the forty-acre site is home to an active museum and outdoor memorials, including an impressive Vietnam Wall replica that is 80 percent the size of the original one in Washington, D.C. Displays inside the museum include war-era uniforms, weapons, photographs, flags and memorabilia from the American Revolution to the Gulf Wars.

The museum has several interesting and unusual artifacts for World War II enthusiasts. A Japanese surrender flyer is one of the unique items with local significance. When Japan surrendered in August 1945, both Fort Wayne newspapers were on strike. Local radio station WGL 1450 printed flyers announcing the surrender and encouraging people to tune in on their radio station for more information. The station hired Margaret Ray Ringenberg, a former Women Airforce Service Pilot (WASP), to fly a plane over downtown and drop fifty-six thousand copies of the flyer from the sky. She was pleased to do so, and through her efforts the residents of Fort Wayne were informed of the war's end.[56] Bud Mendenhall, a Korean war veteran and member of the museum's board of directors, was nine years old at the time of the war's end. He was downtown the day that Ringenberg made her historic air drop and recalled seeing the flyers floating down from the sky.[57]

Ringenberg was a Fort Wayne native who became interested in aviation as an eight-year-old girl. She took flying lessons when she got older and obtained her civilian pilot license at the age of nineteen. In 1943, she joined the WASPs and helped ferry and test new and repaired military aircraft. Ringenberg became a flight instructor when the WASP corps was disbanded at the end of 1944. She continued her avocation with airplanes after the war and participated in air races from 1957 to 2008. She died in 2008 at the age of eighty-seven.[58]

Military art is another interesting display in the museum. World War II veteran and Fort Wayne native Harvey Richard Jessup used the aluminum pieces of downed aircraft to fashion jewelry for his girlfriend and future wife, Doris Lucille Jones of Hicksville, Ohio. Jessup was born on April 18, 1921, in Fort Wayne. He joined the army in 1942 and served with a 155mm Howitzer artillery unit for thirty-nine months in the Province of Batanes, a chain of islands located between Formosa (present-day Taiwan) and Luzon, Philippines. When parts of Japanese aircraft shot down by him and his unit floated by, he secured and used them to create aluminum jewelry for Doris. On display in the museum are a ring, a bracelet and a necklace piece. Each item was crafted around a centerpiece heart. He also created a jewelry canister made from bamboo with a decorative ring around the edge of the lid. Upon Jessup's return from the service, he married Doris on January 1, 1946. He died at the age of eighty in 2002.[59]

Another interesting item from World War II is a blood chit from the China-Burma-India theater. Given to airmen who flew in the 14th Volunteer Bomb Group or the Flying Tigers with the American Volunteer Group, the seven-and-a-half-by-nine-and-a-half-inch silk or cloth chit was sewn on jackets or folded and kept in pilots' pockets. Derived from the Chinese phrase for "life payment," the chits were promises for payment or reward. There were variations in the design of the blood chit. The one in the museum is made of leather and consists of four panels: a U.S. flag, a Nationalist China flag, an emblem for the China-Burma-India theater and Chinese characters that identified the pilots as Allied airmen and asked for help in their evasion and

Military Art WWII

Harvey R. Jessup served 39 months in the U.S. Army in the Baton Islands in the Philippines. He fired at enemy aircraft with a 155mm Howitzer. When pieces of the downed aircraft floated ashore, he created these hand made pieces of jewelry in 1945 for his future wife, Doris Jones of Hicksville, Ohio.

Jewelry made from enemy aircraft pieces by Harvey R. Jessup, Veterans National Memorial Shrine and Museum. *Ronald May*.

New museum and former house of Eric Scott (right), used as the first museum. *Ronald May*.

return. The English translation of the blood chit reads: "This foreign person has come to China to help in the war effort. Soldiers and civilians, one and all, should rescue, protect, and provide him with medical care."[60]

The reopening of the museum, which enjoyed great success in its first four years, has recently expanded to include a new six-thousand-square-foot building. Named the W. Paul Wolf History Museum, the new building provides triple the space of the one housed in the Scotts' old stone home and now displays twice the number of exhibits. The museum's namesake is a Korean War veteran who served in the U.S. Air Force from 1952 to 1956. A supporter of the Veterans National Shrine and Museum, he made a substantial donation for the new museum space. The Scotts' house, first used for the reunion gatherings of the 6th Combat Engineers and formerly used for the museum, has become a banquet and lecture hall for special events. The entrance room has been converted into a Medal of Honor Research Library. Future additions to the site will include building a new Stirling Chapel, with seating for sixty, and a Memorial Columbarium.[61]

Through his own resolve and the help of others, World War I veteran Eric Scott has kept his promise. He would be pleased to see how the museum has grown today and continues to honor the veterans he swore would be remembered.

For more information, visit https://honoringforever.org.

4

ALLEN COUNTY WAR MEMORIAL COLISEUM

Many memorial sites throughout Indiana are visited on special patriotic days like Memorial Day, Independence Day and Veterans Day. The City of Fort Wayne found a way to bring up to thirteen thousand at a time to its memorial site by building a memorial coliseum. Used for major sporting events, entertainment venues, trade shows and exhibitions, the building has been used throughout the year by the people of Allen County for seventy years.

The name of the coliseum, Allen County War Memorial Coliseum, identifies its primary purpose as a living memorial for honoring those who died in service to their country. The coliseum goes well beyond its name in conveying this purpose. Here is the story behind Indiana's largest memorial.

In February 1944, while the United States was still in the middle of World War II, the Fort Wayne Junior Chamber of Commerce proposed the idea of having a coliseum built for the community and using it to memorialize the residents of Allen County, Indiana, who had given their lives in service to the nation during World Wars I and II.[62]

The decision to build a coliseum instead of a memorial statue or monument reflected a trend in the late 1940s to erect "living memorial" structures, places that would serve the needs of the living while also honoring the dead.[63]

The president of the Junior Chamber of Commerce, Paul G. Gronauer, echoed the same sentiment while identifying the coliseum's primary purpose: "War memorials should be for the living, not for the dead alone. The living must be enabled to derive a spiritual lift from them. There must be a shrine to which one may go to commune with the missing and to pay tribute to the returned. A mere building does not serve this purpose. The true memorial building has a heart, a focal point. Some symbol within it must tell why the building was built, and this must be the center of interest."[64] A survey of area residents confirmed wide appeal for erecting a living memorial as 78 percent were in favor of the proposal.[65]

The coliseum's eventual design accomplished both a memorial for the dead and a utilitarian gift for the living. Initial plans called for a fieldhouse that could seat 7,500 and have adequate space for parking. Projected activities in the fieldhouse included basketball, ice skating, large dances, auto shows and trade exhibits.[66] It was decided later in the design phase to expand the seating capacity to accommodate 10,000 people.[67]

The project was brought to the Board of Allen County Commissioners in September 1946. A county referendum vote was held on November 6, 1946, and the resolution for the War Memorial Coliseum, which included an increase of property taxes and a bond issue for financing the coliseum, passed five to one. A County War Memorial Coliseum Commission was formed to help bring the project to fulfillment. A desirable building site consisting of seventy-seven acres, known as the McKay property, was selected north of the downtown area along Parnell Avenue and near Johnny Appleseed Park. It was purchased on October 20, 1947.[68]

Alvin M. Strauss was hired as the architect for the coliseum, and in April 1948, he shared his preliminary plans with the planning committee and the county commissioners.[69] In December 1949, the construction contract was awarded to the Hagerman Construction Company, whose bid for the project was just under $2 million.[70] The price later rose to $3 million.

The groundbreaking ceremony took place on January 24, 1950. Construction proceeded steadily for the next two years. On Memorial Day 1952, the Allen County Council of Veterans Organizations participated in a special flag-raising ceremony in front of the nearly completed building.[71]

Meanwhile, efforts had been ongoing to get a complete list of the Allen County residents who had died in service to their country during World War I or II so that their names could be included on the memorial plaques that would hang in the coliseum's Memorial Hall. This special room honoring the war dead would become the heart of the structure. A final list of 643 men and women appeared on the honor roll.[72] Later, new plaques were added to include the names of those who died in Korea and Vietnam. More recently, space has been designated for a Persian Gulf War Honor Roll.

Memorial Hall, Allen County War Memorial Coliseum. *Ronald May*.

In September 1952, eight years after the idea was first proposed, the Allen County War Memorial Coliseum was completed. A city-wide celebratory dedication ceremony was held on September 28 and was preceded by a parade in which area high school bands and twenty-four county veterans' organizations participated. The coliseum was packed to capacity, with ten thousand attendees for the official dedication program.[73]

The completed coliseum was massive for the time, rising 425 feet in height and extending 300 feet in length. The whole structure was a showcase of architectural genius and elegance. Indiana limestone and brick adorned the exterior of the octagonal structure.[74]

The coliseum's Memorial Hall was created with distinction both inside and outside.

Five cast aluminum heads have been placed on the exterior of the building above the windows of the hall. These heads symbolize the Army, Navy, Marine Corps, Coast Guard, and Air Force. The interior of the august hall measures seventy-five feet in length and thirty feet in width. Four kinds of marble are used in the decoration: French Notre Dame for the background, English Renfrew for the inserts, Italian Red Levanto for the platform, and Spanish Bois Jourdan for the door panels. Two bronze plaques, one at either end of the hall, list the casualties of Allen County beneath the following

Aluminum heads of service branches over Memorial Hall Entrance, Allen County War Memorial Coliseum. *Ronald May.*

> *inscription: "This Coliseum is dedicated as a living memorial in honor of these men and women who gave their lives in World Wars I and II of the nation so that we might live."* [75]

Each name on the bronze plaques is that of a local son or daughter from Allen County who served in World War I or II. There are 643 names and 643 individual stories behind each of those names, the common thread being that they all died while in service to the nation.[76]

Arthur Glenn's name is among those listed under the World War II section of the plaque. His service story began during World War I and abruptly concluded during the first hours of America's forced entrance into World War II.

Glenn was born on December 7, 1898, in Lonaconing, Maryland. Sometime after 1910, the Glenn family moved to Fort Wayne, Indiana.[77] After graduating from high school, Glenn enlisted in the U.S. Navy on April 12, 1917, six days after the U.S. entrance into the war. He served on several different ships.

At war's end, Glenn decided to make the navy a career. He served for the next twenty-four years on ships in both the Atlantic and Pacific Oceans and rose from a seaman to the rank of a first-class petty officer machinist's mate.[78]

Arthur Glenn, *center*, in uniform. *Matt Glenn.*

On December 7, 1941, the date of his forty-third birthday, Glenn was serving on the USS *Oklahoma*, which was stationed at Pearl Harbor, Hawaii. Shortly before 8:00 a.m., Japanese aircraft began dropping bombs and torpedoes on the ships along battleship row. Several torpedoes struck the USS *Oklahoma*. It capsized within twelve minutes. The surprise attack killed 429 of its crew members, including MM1C Arthur Glenn. His unidentified remains were buried along with hundreds of other unknowns in the National Memorial Cemetery of the Pacific on Oahu.[79]

In 2017, Arthur Glenn's remains were finally identified using DNA testing with members of his extended family. On August 21, 2018, a full seventy-six years after he was killed, his remains were reinterred with other USS *Oklahoma* shipmates in a ceremony that included full military honors at the National Memorial Cemetery of the Pacific at Punchbowl Crater in Honolulu. Members of Glenn's extended family attended.[80]

The coliseum's footprint has expanded several times over the decades following the original structure's completion. An exposition center was added in 1989 along with a new entrance rotunda. In 2001, the arena underwent a renovation that included raising the roof, installing luxury suites and increasing the seating capacity to thirteen thousand. And in 2015,

Veterans Plaza in front of Memorial Hall, Allen County War Memorial Coliseum. *Allen County War Memorial Coliseum. John McGauley.*

a conference center was erected, bringing the coliseum's footprint to more than 1 million square feet and making it the second-largest public gathering facility in the state of Indiana.[81]

True to its original purpose, memorial elements in the coliseum grew as well during the expansions. Bronze sculptures of three military figures, created by Loveland, Colorado artist Ann LaRose, were placed in the Expo's rotunda entrance in 1990. The sculpture consists of a Continental army figure from the Revolutionary War period, a female in uniform from the World War II era and a soldier from the Vietnam War. The figures are looking up at two other statues: an adult man and a young boy who are standing on the second floor of the expo lobby, looking down at the military statues. The man is saluting the figures, while the boy is waving a handheld flag.

Recognition of veterans expanded to the outside of the coliseum in 2015 with the dedication of a Veterans Plaza in front of the Memorial Hall entrance. The plaza includes an F-84F Thunderstreak plane from the Korean War, the massive anchor from the World War II Battleship USS *Indiana*, an eternal flame and several other memorials.[82]

The most recent veteran honor came in a road name change. In 2021, the section of Parnell Road that passes the main entrance into the coliseum was renamed the Veterans Memorial Mile.[83]

Throughout its seventy years of existence, the Allen County War Memorial Coliseum has stood proudly as a "living memorial" to those who died in service to their country and a tribute to area veterans. Veterans in the region continue to be honored annually with parades that end at the coliseum and special programs in Memorial Hall that take place on Memorial Day, Veterans Day and Pearl Harbor Day.[84]

5

BAER ARMY AIRFIELD

I n 1940, the U.S. War Department was considering sites to build military airfields in Indiana. Typically, the War Department selected the locations for new airfields and then imposed its will on the local landowners to sell the land.[85] In a surprise move, the community leaders of Fort Wayne invited the War Department to build an army air base in their patriotic city.[86]

The city chose seven hundred acres southwest of the city as a prime site for a future airfield in case the War Department elected to build one there. One year later, in January 1941, the War Department contacted the city to accept its offer for land, but its stipulation was that the property had to be available to lease within thirty days. Unable to arrange for the sale of bonds to cover the $125,000 purchase of land that quickly, the progressive-thinking city leaders asked the presidents of four local banks to advance the money needed to buy the property from the landowners. The bank presidents did so with the help of thirty local business leaders who offered notes to the banks for the advance on the purchase.[87]

Construction began, and by June 1941, the new airfield had been named Baer Army Airfield. Although the city had wanted to name the airfield after General Anthony Wayne, the local Revolutionary War hero, the army insisted that the airfield be named for an army flier. The city recommended the name of Paul Baer, a Fort Wayne native who flew combat missions for the army in Europe during World War I. The army agreed, and Baer Army Airfield became the official designation.[88]

The airfield, which included three runways more than one mile long and a small city of one hundred buildings to support the airfield's mission and house base personnel, opened in late 1941. It was initially designated as a fighter training base for P-39 Airacobras of the 31st Pursuit Group. The outbreak of war after the Pearl Harbor attack necessitated that the planes be moved to guard the East Coast, and a few months later, they were moved to England for the buildup of U.S. Army Air Forces units there.[89]

The next fighter group assigned to the base was the P-38 Lightning from the 78th Fighter Group. After a few months, the group departed for desert training in California and then deployed to England to provide escort duty for B-17 bombers. The group was later transferred to the 12th Air Force in North Africa.[90]

For a short time in August 1942, the base was assigned to the Foreign Service Concentration Command and handled the processing of the B-26 medium bombers. This involved running a multitude of tests on the planes that had just come off the production lines. More than three hundred bombers were processed through Baer Field from September 1942 through June 1943.[91] Many of these same bombers were used in the Battle of Midway.[92]

In March 1943, the base was assigned to I Troop Carrier Command. The airfield's new mission was crew processing and combat training of troop carrier groups flying the C-46 Commando and C-47 Skytrain

Baer Field Airport postcard.

Douglas C-47 Skytrain, Fort Campbell, Kentucky, July 12, 2013. *Gary Todd.*

transport planes. The planes were thoroughly inspected and tested by Baer Field personnel, and final changes were made to the aircraft, which often included installing long-range fuel tanks before deploying them for overseas missions.[93]

Native Hoosier Robert E. Tangeman was among the thousands of carrier group crewmembers who passed through Baer Army Airfield on their way to combat theaters.[94] An Indianapolis boy and Shortridge High School graduate, Tangeman enlisted in the U.S. Army Air Forces and was inducted at Fort Benjamin Harrison in late November 1942. Following his basic training in Miami Beach, Florida, he attended aircraft mechanic school in Gulfport, Mississippi, graduating in May 1943. He was then sent to the Douglas Aircraft Plant in Long Beach, California, for familiarization training with the C-47 "Skytrain" transports that were built there.[95]

Tangeman arrived at Baer Army Air Base in the summer of 1943 and spent a week training with the 81st Troop Carrier Squadron, the unit to which he had been assigned. His next stop was Alliance Field, Nebraska, where he met up with his C-47 plane and crew. They departed for final squadron training at Laurinburg-Maxton Field in North Carolina. The crew returned briefly to Baer Army Air Base for final processing before overseas deployment. One week later, Tangeman's crew headed to Camp Shanks, New York, to prepare for final departure to the European Theater.[96]

The 81st Troop Carrier Squadron was assigned to the Royal Air Force Base in Membury, England (sixty miles west of London), in Berkshire, where it remained throughout 1944. It was part of the 9th Air Force in England. The squadron supported both the 101st and 82nd Airborne Divisions, carrying both paratroopers and gliders to drop zones during the invasion of Normandy in June 1944 and during Operation Market Garden in Holland in September 1944.[97]

Tangeman was promoted to assistant crew chief and helped oversee all maintenance work on his crew's transport plane, making sure that it was always ready for its missions. Although he didn't accompany the flight crew for every mission, he did go on some of them.[98]

In February 1945, the 81st Troop Carrier Squadron moved to Airbase A-55 in France, just south of Paris. Tangeman went on a dozen flights into Germany during the spring, resupplying American forces. By July 1945, he had returned home and received an honorable discharge.[99]

In early 1944, while Tangeman was in Europe, Baer Army Airfield's mission expanded. It began refurbishing aircraft that had returned from combat service overseas. These planes were inspected, repaired and sometimes overhauled.[100]

Lieutenant Robert Kearns, who had grown up in Indiana, was one of the hundreds of C-47 pilots who stopped at Baer Army Airfield in January 1945 to be issued gear on his way to the combat theater.[101] "We were sent to Fort Wayne, Indiana, to get our gear to go overseas," Kearns explained in a 2006 interview for the Library of Congress Veterans History Project. "We got our fur-lined flying suits, boots, and hats, and all our gear, and we were sent to Seattle. By the time we got to Seattle, we had a pretty good idea we weren't going to go to Europe." They headed instead across the Pacific Ocean on troop transports.[102]

Lieutenant Robert Kearns, Alliance Army Air Base, Nebraska, April 1944. *Robert Kearns.*

Kearns was stationed at Harmon Airfield on the island of Guam, and instead of pulling gliders, he flew his C-47 on supply and medical evacuation missions to Iwo Jima, which had been taken by the Marine Corps at the end of March 1945. Following Japan's surrender in September, Kearns flew occupation troops into Japan. For the next nine months, he was kept busy flying dignitaries and VIPs from Guam to Japan. He witnessed firsthand, both from the air and on the ground, the destruction from the atomic bombs that had been dropped on Hiroshima and Nagasaki. He returned to the United States in May 1946 and was discharged.[103]

While Kearns was flying missions between Guam and Japan in the last months of the war, Baer Army Airfield served as an assembly station for plane crews returning from combat service in Europe to prepare for deployment to the Pacific Theater.[104] With the surrender of Japan in September 1945, many of those crews were spared from having to leave the country again.

Baer Field was put into inactive status at the end of December 1945, four months after Japan signed the surrender documents. It served briefly as a separation center to discharge returning service members. The airfield was returned to the city of Fort Wayne in March 1946 and began its new mission as the Fort Wayne Municipal Airport, eventually adopting the name of Fort Wayne International Airport.[105]

During its four years as an army air base, Baer Field trained hundreds of pilots, serviced hundreds of planes and was a duty station for 100,000 military personnel.[106]

In 1984 and for the next thirty-six years, the Fort Wayne International Airport hosted exhibits for the Greater Fort Wayne Aviation Museum, which included items from its early history as Baer Army Airfield. The exhibits were removed in 2020. Today, some of those items from the exhibits can be found in the History Center of Fort Wayne and the Veterans National Memorial Shrine and Museum, also in Fort Wayne.

Throughout the war, the Fort Wayne community maintained a healthy partnership with Baer Field and the personnel assigned to it. The city enjoyed the special pride of knowing that it had been the catalyst for the airfield's existence, which had made a significant contribution to the war effort.

The air force continues to have a presence in Fort Wayne. An Indiana Air National Guard Fighter Group was activated in May 1946 and assigned to Stout Field in Indianapolis. Renamed the 122nd Fighter Wing in 1952, it was relocated to the old Baer Army Airfield in 1954. The air wing occupies part of the Fort Wayne International Airport today.[107]

In 2013, a public park was created just outside the entrance to the base. Named the 122nd Fighter Wing Heritage Park, it showcases aircraft that the Indiana Air National Guard has flown since 1947.[108] And, indirectly, it serves as a tribute to the men and aircraft that once served at Baer Army Airfield during World War II.

6

NAVAL AIR STATION BUNKER HILL AND GRISSOM AIR MUSEUM

Following the attack at Pearl Harbor and the U.S. entrance into the war, the Department of the Navy scrambled to identify sites and build air stations across the country to train aviation cadets for the war effort. The Naval Air Station Bunker Hill became one of twenty-four such stations built during 1942 and 1943.[109]

Some two thousand acres of prime farmland in North Central Indiana along Highway 31, eighteen miles north of Kokomo and seven miles south of Peru, were selected by navy officials in February 1942 for one of their new air stations.[110]

The location offered exactly what navy planners were looking for: flat topography to build runways, low population density, significant distance away from other airports, access to railroad lines and proximity to other key midwestern cities like Chicago, Detroit, Cincinnati and Indianapolis.[111]

The plans for the air station called for four runways of five thousand feet and space for 1,200 aviation students and 1,500 base personnel.[112] Building the air station required 64 landowners to sell their property to the U.S. government.[113]

A massive Water Survival Training Pool was built, reaching two stories high and descending into a partial basement. The height of the pool building was designed to approximate the height from the open sea to the deck of an aircraft carrier. "Abandon ship" and lifeboat drills were practiced by jumping off the wooden boards secured to ladders high above the pool.[114]

Another key building on base was the Link Trainer Building, which held sixteen Link Trainers.[115] These compressed models of a plane's cockpit were flight simulators attached to a lift mechanism that moved the cockpit up and down as well as sideways while students practiced flying by instrument navigation.

Just seven months after the events at Pearl Harbor, the U.S. Naval Reserve Aviation Base, Peru, was commissioned on July 1, 1942. The name for the base changed to Naval Air Station Peru in January 1943 and became the Naval Air Station (NAS) Bunker Hill two months later in March 1943, a name it would keep for the remaining duration of the war.[116]

Additional construction, base personnel, aviation students and training operations expanded at a rapid pace following its commissioning. The first group of aviation students arrived at NAS Bunker Hill on September 20, 1942. They had just completed their preflight training at the University of North Carolina.[117]

The flight training for naval aviation cadets at the beginning of the war involved three stages. The first was Pre-Flight training, which was all academic, lasted twelve weeks and took place at one of six universities located in California, Georgia, Iowa and North Carolina. The second stage was Primary Flight Training, which took place at Bunker Hill or one of the other Primary Training sites: Glenview, Illinois; New Orleans, Louisiana; Norman, Oklahoma; Ottumwa, Iowa; or Dallas, Texas. Primary Training lasted twelve weeks and involved instruction in basic flying as well

NAS Bunker Hill Tarmac and Control Tower, 1943. *Miami County Museum.*

as navigation, radio communication and engine familiarity. Intermediate Flight, which focused on combat training, was the third stage. Depending on the type of plane flown, the training was held either at the Naval Air Station Corpus Christi, Texas, or in Pensacola, Florida.[118] A strenuous physical fitness regimen was maintained through all the cycles of training.

Upon arrival at Bunker Hill, cadets were assigned to one of two flight wings. Training consisted of classroom learning, physical fitness and flying. Flight training included flying with an instructor, flying solo, flying cross country, flying in formation, flying at night, instrument flying and the beginning of aerobatic flying. Cadets spent time in the Link Trainers to become familiar with instrument flying.[119]

The training plane used most often at the Primary Flight Training bases was the N2S-3, Kaydet biplane, also known as a Stearman. An open-cockpit two-seater (for an instructor and student), it was built by Boeing-Stearman. It was just under twenty-five feet long and reached up in height to more than nine and a half feet. The plane had a wingspan of almost twenty-five feet, could fly for 505 miles and reached speeds of up to 135 miles per hour while cruising to an altitude of thirteen thousand feet. It was the entry-level plane for cadets in both the U.S. Army Air Forces and the U.S. Navy.[120] More than four hundred of these planes were used at NAS Bunker Hill during the peak of training.[121]

While the aviation cadets spent many hours in the biplanes, the flight instructors had even more time in them. Joseph Edward Durnin Sr. was one of those instructors. A Pennsylvania native, Durnin held both a bachelor's and master's degree in chemistry. He was working for Bethlehem Steel as a metallurgist when the United States entered the war.[122]

Commissioned in the navy in November 1942 at the age of twenty-seven, he attended Flight Training at Bucknell University, earning his certificate as a naval aviator in August 1943. Following Flight Instructor's School at Bloomsburg, Pennsylvania, he had additional training at the Naval Air Stations in Glenview, Illinois, and New Orleans, Louisiana, before arriving at NAS Bunker Hill on August 29, 1943. He spent the next twenty-one months as a primary flight instructor, likely training more than one hundred cadets.[123]

While he undoubtedly had some favorite cadets, he held one in his highest esteem: Boston Red Sox star baseball player Ted Williams.[124] Williams, who reported along with fellow ballplayer Johnny Pesky, arrived at NAS Bunker Hill in September 1943. The duo had earned number one and two hitting records in 1942 in the American League.[125]

Joe Durnin in front of the Stearman plane. *Rene Williams, daughter of Joe Durnin.*

Williams and Pesky were two of Durnin's first cadets. "He was the best flyer I ever met," Durnin said of Williams in a conversation with his children. "Great hand and eye coordination!"[126] Both Williams and Pesky were popular during their twelve weeks at Bunker Hill, and both, although wealthy sports stars by this point, acted like regular guys. They put their hand and eye coordination skills to good use in flying the planes. Both left for their final flight training in Pensacola in December 1943. Williams said of his twelve weeks at Bunker Hill, "It's a grand place and a grand bunch of guys."[127]

Williams later showed his own grandness and fondness for his old aviation instructor when, after the war ended and he returned to playing baseball, he gave free tickets to Durnin so that he could attend games when the Red Sox were in New York City.[128]

Although Williams and Pesky were easily the most well-known cadets at Bunker Hill, there were other new faces that also attracted some attention—female faces. In June 1943, a group of Navy WAVES (Women Accepted for Volunteer Service) arrived on base to serve as yeomen. They were soon joined by WAVES trained as machinists. Within a year, the number of women serving in uniform as WAVES at Bunker Hill grew to more than three hundred. They contributed greatly to the base's mission by operating

Link Trainers, assisting in the control tower, packing parachutes, maintaining plane engines, working in supply, maintaining personnel records and helping with disbursement.[129]

The cadet community gained international status when British cadets from the Royal Navy began arriving for Primary Flight Training at the base in August 1944. Early in the war, Royal Navy leaders decided to send their cadets to the safer skies of the United States for pilot training so that they could avoid the disruptions from German air attacks over England. More than eight hundred British cadets eventually passed through Bunker Hill during the war.[130]

By the end of March 1945, some 5,997 American cadets had begun primary training at NAS Bunker Hill. The results of the training were impressive: 4,568 (76 percent) successfully completed the twelve-week training and advanced to intermediate flight training, while 854 cadets (14 percent attrition) washed out of the program and were either sent home with a discharge or transferred for reclassification to Great Lakes Naval Training Station. A smaller group of 25 cadets were transferred to naval hospitals to continue their recovery from injury or illness.[131]

The worst of the statistics, although thankfully a small number, was the nine cadets who died in plane crashes during their training. Six of the fatalities occurred in 1943 and another three in 1944. Each was a sad reminder of the inherent danger of students and instructors taking to the sky to train for aerial warfare.[132]

In the fall of 1945, the beehive of training stopped almost as quickly as it had started. At war's end, the Naval Air Station Bunker Hill was quickly decommissioned. The *Kokomo Tribune* reported as early as September 4, 1945, that the navy had announced plans to close the base by December 1, 1945. Cadets who were still in the middle of their training were given the option to discharge and return to civilian life or seek a transfer to another base.[133] By February 1946, four years after it had been chosen by the navy to become an air station, much of the footprint of NAS Bunker Hill had reverted back to farmland.[134]

In 1954, eight years after the base's closing, the air force took control of the former Naval Air Station at Bunker Hill. Initially, it was called the Bunker Hill Air Force Base, but the name was changed in 1968 to Grissom Air Force Base in memory of native Hoosier astronaut Virgil "Gus" Grissom, who was a veteran flyer in both World War II and Korea and lost his life in 1967 while serving as pilot of Apollo 1. In 1994, the base was reduced in size and operation due to a 1991 Base Realignment and Closure (BRAC) decision. It

Grissom Air Museum, outdoor display of planes viewed from the observation tower. *Ronald May.*

became an Air Force Reserve station, and its name was tweaked to Grissom Air Reserve Base. It continues in that capacity today and is home to a KC-135R Stratotanker wing in the Air Force Reserve.[135]

GRISSOM AIR MUSEUM

On the north side of the reserve base is the Grissom Air Museum, which opened in 1987. Twenty historic aircraft are displayed in a large outdoor area in front of the museum, including a World War II–era B-25 bomber. By climbing the steps of the old observation tower, one can take in a panoramic view of all the planes and see in the distance the area that once was the Navy Air Station at Bunker Hill and later became an air force base.

Inside the museum, there are many interesting displays and artifacts from the base's early history as a Naval Air Station to its more recent history of being a U.S. Air Force and Air Force Reserve installation. It is worth the stop to see it.

For more information, visit https://www.grissomairmuseum.com.

7

BLUE/GOLD STAR FAMILY AND WOMEN'S LEGACY MEMORIALS

Howard County, Indiana, honors its veterans, the men and women who have served, endured and contributed to the nation's welfare. More than that, it honors their families, for they also have made significant sacrifices.

The Howard County Veterans Memorial is located inside Veterans Memorial Park on the east side of the city of Kokomo, the county seat. Like many county memorials honoring their veterans, it is a fine tribute to all those who have served their country.

What makes Howard County Veterans Memorial Park truly unique, however, is the memorial to families of military members built just to the east of the veterans' memorial. Named the Blue/Gold Star Family Memorial, it pays tribute to all the Howard County families whose sons and daughters have served in the armed forces, some of whom never returned home again.

The memorial was the brainchild of Kokomo resident Jerry Paul, a Vietnam War veteran. Paul, president of the Howard County Veterans Memorial Corporation board, came up with the design for the memorial in 2010 after ideas submitted by community members failed to gain traction.[136]

The memorial features two bronze sculptures facing each other but separated by thirty-five feet across an empty concrete pad. On the north end of the memorial is a family consisting of a husband, his wife and their child. With sad faces, they look to the south.

Blue/Gold Star Family Memorial, with soldier reaching toward his family, Kokomo. *Ronald May.*

The husband, standing behind his wife, has both of his hands resting on her shoulders. The wife/mother is stretching her left arm forward, toward the object of her attention. Her right arm reaches down to the back of her daughter who stands beside her, resting her head on her mother's hip.

The object of their focus, standing thirty-five feet in front of them, is their grown son/brother in a military uniform. He is looking back at them with similarly longing eyes. His right arm extends out in front of him, and his open hand reveals the desire to connect with his family. He is in the uniform of a marine, a rifle slung over his left shoulder. Behind him is a brick wall with the seals of each branch of the U.S. Armed Forces. The pain of separation is clearly and powerfully conveyed by the placement of the two sculptures apart from yet facing each other.

During a 2015 interview with Laura Slagter of the *Kokomo Tribune*, Paul said of his memorial's intent, "We need to remember, it's not just those who serve. It's those who support and sacrifice to protect our nation."[137] The family members and the lone marine symbolize all family units who have been separated from their sons and daughters while they perform their military service, often far from home.

During the years of World War II, 16 million Americans left their families behind and served in places far from their loved ones. They were separated for long periods, sometimes years. Many of them fought hostile enemies in different countries. And some of them, more than 450,000 during World War II, did not return home alive.

Blue and Gold Star is the title for the family memorial. The terms hearken back to the days when blue and gold stars were sewn on flags to denote sons or daughters who were away from home serving in the military (blue stars) and those who had died while serving their nation (gold stars). Conceived during World War I, the white flags with a red border became even more popular during World War II when 16 million sons and daughters left home for military service.

Paul Maves was one of those World War II service members. The Lyons, Illinois native served with the 8th Air Force as a bombardier on B-26 medium bombers in England and France. While he was deployed to Europe, his parents kept a service flag hung from the front window of their home in Lyons in honor of Maves.[138]

After the death of his parents, Maves, who moved to Speedway, Indiana, in 1965, kept the flag that once hung for him in his parents' home. Although faded by time, it was clear how much the flag had meant not only to his parents but also to Maves himself. He passed the flag on to his children following his death in 2020.

The Blue/Gold Star Family Memorial rightly leaves a sad impression on the viewer. That was sculptor Benjamin Victor's intention. "I hope they feel

Paul Maves with the service star flag passed down from his parents, 2012. *Ronald May*.

that distance," said the Boise, Idaho artist in the 2015 interview. "The family, they're here, they're missing that loved one and there's the anxiety of, 'Are they coming back?' and also that loss."[139]

But the stronger impression of the memorial is devotion, as both the family and the marine are reaching toward the other. Their love for each other spans the separation they must endure. Even when there is no way to connect physically, it is clear in their reaching out to each other that their hearts are already connected. And nothing, not distance nor death, can break that connection.

Five years after the Blue/Gold Star Family Memorial was dedicated, Jerry Paul was the catalyst for another memorial in his hometown of Kokomo. This one honors the women who have served at home as well as those who entered the service in one of the armed forces.

The Indiana Women's Legacy Memorial was dedicated in August 2021. Located on the northeast corner of the Howard County Courthouse in downtown Kokomo, the memorial sculptures were also created by Benjamin Victor, the same sculptor for the Blue/Gold Star Family Memorial.

This memorial consists of three bronze statues of women on pedestals of various heights. One woman, a female soldier in a contemporary uniform,

Indiana Women's Legacy Memorial, Kokomo. *Ronald May.*

is kneeling with her head slightly bowed. Her right hand is placed over her heart in devotion, and her left hand holds an old musket. The word *DUTY* is engraved on her pedestal. Her left pant leg is rolled up, revealing a prosthetic leg. She represents all women who have served and are serving in today's armed forces.[140]

Behind her stands a female aviator in her flying suit, holding her helmet in her left arm. She is a woman of color, symbolizing the many women of different races who have served in uniform. The statue depicts Shawna Rochelle Kimbrell, who was born in Lafayette, Indiana, and in 2000 became the first female African American fighter pilot to serve in the Air Force. *HONOR* is the pedestal she stands on.[141]

The final figure is a woman in work clothes wearing a head wrap and flexing her arm in the iconic pose for strength. She is a Rosie the Riveter, symbolizing all women who have worked on the homefront to support their families and nation. Her pedestal is labeled *FAITH*.

During World War II, more than 16 million fathers, husbands and sons left their homes to serve in the armed forces. Their departure created critical shortages in the labor force. More than 6 million women stepped up to fill those vacancies in factories across the United States, most of which had been converted to wartime production. Several million women volunteered with the American Red Cross or United Service Organization.[142] Another 350,000 women entered military service by joining one of the women's auxiliary branches.[143]

Betty (Mitchell) Robling of Mooresville, Indiana, was one of the Rosies during World War II. Robling was a Bridgeport, Illinois native. Born on April 7, 1924, she graduated from Bridgeport High School in 1943. After graduating, she learned that Republic Airlines in Evansville, Indiana, was hiring women to help build the P-47 fighter aircraft. She moved to Evansville that same year and became a riveter. "I weighed only 95 pounds and sat at a table with a vice where I placed rivets into small sheets of metal used for different parts of the plane," she recalled in an interview with the author. Robling's work involved putting rivets into pre-drilled holes and then bucking the ends of them until they pressed down to the other piece of metal.[144]

Robling and the other 6 million women like her not only contributed to the war effort by entering the workforce, but they also helped pave the way for future generations of women to pursue careers while also raising families.[145]

Behind the statues of the Women's Legacy Memorial in Kokomo is a large stone pillar with a blue state of Indiana and these words:

> INDIANA
> *Women's Legacy Memorial*
> *This memorial is dedicated to Hoosier Daughters for their time in service to*
> *our state and nation during war and peace.*
> *May their deeds not be forgotten.*

Thanks to Jerry Paul and the creative work of Benjamin Victor, the contributions of women and the sacrifices of their families will not be easily forgotten by those who pass by the memorials.

8

MUSEUM OF THE SOLDIER

The Coca-Cola Company played a role during World War II for Americans serving overseas. Today, a former Coca-Cola bottling company in Portland, Indiana, preserves the history and stories of some area residents who served in that war.

When the United States entered World War II in 1941, Robert Woodruff, president of the Coca-Cola Company, made a pledge "to see that every man in uniform gets a bottle of Coca-Cola for five cents, wherever he is and whatever it costs the company." The company went to extraordinary efforts to make good on that pledge in 1943 by shipping not only 3 million bottles of Coca-Cola but also equipment and supplies to establish ten bottling operations in North Africa. The feat was later expanded to establish fifty-four other bottling plants throughout the theaters of operation, which ultimately produced 5 billion bottles of Coca-Cola for U.S. Armed Forces personnel serving abroad.[146]

Back home, Portland, Indiana, the county seat of Jay County, was producing its own supply of the popular beverage in its brick bottling plant located on the corner of East Arch and North Hayes Streets. The plant, which had been in operation since 1919, kept residents supplied with Coca-Cola throughout the tumultuous war years. Portland's plant operation eventually relocated to a different location in the town, leaving behind a vacant building and an opportunity for three local men to open a museum of war memorabilia.

James Waechter, Brian Williamson and Michael McBride had been collecting items and providing displays for schools and local events from the early 1980s. People who saw the traveling exhibits kept asking them where their museum was located. They had to reply that there was no home for their museum. That all changed when the closed bottling plant became available. In 1997, the Hondo Inc. corporation and its parent company of Coca-Cola gifted the former bottling plant to the Museum of the Soldier Inc., which had been created by the three men as a nonprofit organization. The Museum of the Soldier finally had a home.[147]

The building that once held the popular beverage now holds some of the memorabilia and stories of those who drank the product in war theaters. The displays feature many former service members from Jay County and are portals for learning more of each person's service and, often, sacrifice.

Herbert K. Bubp, a native son of Portland, is one of those stories. The Sons in Service Flag from the Bubp family hangs from one of the display partitions. It has four blue stars in the field of white, noting that their four sons were all serving in the armed forces in World War II. One of those stars, representing Herbert, was destined for gold thread, representing a son killed in action.

Museum of the Soldier. *Ronald May.*

Bubp, who was born in 1921 and graduated from Portland High School in 1941, enlisted in the navy in October 1942. After completing boot camp at Great Lakes Naval Training Center, he attended diesel training school in Richmond, Virginia, and then submarine school in New London, Connecticut. Bubp was assigned to the newly built USS *Cisco* (SS-290) submarine, which had been commissioned for service on May 10, 1943. He was a fireman first class responsible for firing and tending the boilers, as well as operating, adjusting and repairing the pumps in the submarine.[148]

Prior to departing for service overseas, he married Dorothy Brinckerhoff, another Portland native, on May 8, 1943. The couple moved to Battle Creek, Michigan, after their wedding so Dorothy could be closer to her sister when Bubp deployed.[149]

The *Cisco* left its homeport on July 24, 1943, for the Panama Canal zone. It arrived in Brisbane, Australia, on September 2 and, following some operational exercises, departed Darwin, Australia, on September 20 for its first war patrol. Its orders were to patrol the South China Sea.[150]

On September 28, an oil slick on the surface of the water was discovered by Japanese planes, which coordinated with Japanese ships to launch depth charge attacks on the *Cisco*. A large gush of oil on the water's surface confirmed that it had been fatally hit. Later attempts by the Headquarters of Task Force Seventy-One to establish radio contact with *Cisco* failed, and it was presumed lost.[151] The navy officially declared the ship lost at sea on February 8, 1944.

Herbert Bubp, age twenty-two, just nine days into his first submarine patrol in enemy waters, died in service to his country along with the rest of the crew of seventy-six.[152] He left behind his widow, Dorothy; his parents; and his brothers, all of whom survived the war. Herbert K. Bubp's name and the words "Buried at Sea" appear on the headstone of his parents at Green Park Cemetery in Portland, Indiana.[153]

Bubp was not the only native Hoosier on board the *Cisco* at the time of its sinking. The commanding officer of the submarine, Commander James W. Coe, was a native of Richmond, Indiana. The Naval Academy graduate served on four submarines during a ten-year stretch, scoring multiple hits on Japanese vessels. He was a veteran skipper with six patrols under his belt.[154] His wife, Rachel, gave birth to their third child, a daughter, Mary Lee, in April, just six months after he departed on *Cisco* for Australia.[155]

Other stories of service and sacrifice by Jay County and area sons during World War II abound in the museum.

Milo "Bill" Ludy of Portland was one of the first men to die on D-Day, June 6, 1944, when the C-47 cargo plane that was carrying him and others from the 501st Parachute Infantry Division was hit by enemy fire and burst into flames, killing Ludy and many others. His Purple Heart and personal letters are on display in the museum.[156]

Five weeks after D-Day, Jay County native PFC John Carder of Redkey, Indiana, was killed in action during the fighting in St. Lo, France. He was assigned to the 134th Infantry Regiment in the 35th Infantry Division. The display on Carder includes letters to his brother, an ensign in the navy, and to other family members.[157]

A service dress blue uniform of Don F. Gardner, also of Portland, is another display of local interest. The chief motor machinist mate first class had plenty of close calls with death, but he managed to escape each time. Serving with Motor Torpedo Boat Squadron 10 in the Pacific Theater, he had the unlikely distinction of surviving attacks while on five different torpedo boats that were lost in action in the South Pacific. He received a Purple Heart for injuries he sustained on one of those attacks.[158]

Displays with letters, photographs, medals, plaques and uniforms bear witness to many other native Hoosiers who served during World War II and other wars.

The back of the museum features some larger military items, including an impressive restoration of a 1943 White M16A2 Half-Track vehicle with

1943 White M16A2 Half-Track. *Ronald May.*

a multiple gun motor carriage. Named the *African Queen*, the vehicle served in the European Theater during World War II and saw service in Korea, French Indochina and Africa. It was abandoned in Africa and sat there for fifty years until 2006, when it was finally recovered and painstakingly restored. It is a marvel to see.[159]

In addition to personal service stories, the exhibits pertaining to World War II include weapons, vehicles and a Norden bomb sight. The Museum of the Soldier also has many fine exhibits from the Civil War to the more recent War on Terrorism.

The former Coca-Cola bottling plant in Portland is no longer just a historic building reminding people of the beverage once bottled there—it is a gold mine of military history that specializes in preserving the stories of men and women from Northeast Indiana who served in our nation's armed forces in times of war. And for that, we can raise a bottle of the popular soda to toast the men who brought the museum to life.

For more information, visit http://museumofthesoldier.info.

PART II

CENTRAL INDIANA

9

ERNIE PYLE
WORLD WAR II MUSEUM

Dana, a small town in Vermillion County, Indiana, near the Illinois border off U.S. 36 and bisecting Central Indiana, has fewer than seven hundred residents. It would be easy to miss the town on a map and still easier never to pass it in your travels. But it would be a mistake to not stop here, for the town has a prominent place in World War II history. It is the birthplace of Ernie Pyle, the most well-known and loved correspondent who covered the war. Today, the town is home to the Ernie Pyle World War II Museum, which features the farmhouse where Pyle was born and two World War II–era Quonset huts filled with exhibits tracing his dispatch coverage of World War II.

Pyle, born in 1900, was raised on a farm outside of Dana. He was the only child of his parents, who gave him the name Ernest Taylor Pyle. Pyle's young life was immersed in the hard-work culture of farming, which did not suit the wanderlust that grew inside of Pyle. He wanted to get out of rural Indiana and see the world.[160]

He hoped that his ticket off the farm would come through military service in World War I. Following his graduation from Bono High School in 1918, he enlisted in the U.S. Naval Reserve. But to Pyle's disappointment, the war ended prior to the completion of his training, and he was discharged.[161]

Determined to stay away from farming, Pyle enrolled at Indiana University in Bloomington in the fall of 1919 and began taking classes in journalism. By his sophomore year, he was writing for the school's newspaper, the *Indiana Daily Student*. Reporting for the newspaper introduced him to his life's vocation

Ernie Pyle Childhood Home and Museum. *Ronald May.*

and satisfied his desire for travel while accompanying the university's sports teams for their away games.[162]

Pyle's love for journalism prompted him to leave the university midway through his senior year to take a job as a reporter with the *LaPorte Herald* in Northern Indiana. His stay there was brief, however, as he soon received a job offer to join the staff of the *Washington Daily News* in the nation's capital.[163] It was there that he met his future wife, Geraldine "Jerry" Siebolds of Minnesota, whom he married in 1925.[164]

Pyle's lust for travel prompted him to quit his reporter job in June 1926 and take Jerry on a ten-week driving adventure across the country in a Ford Model T roadster he had purchased. Upon their return to the East Coast, he briefly worked for two newspapers in New York City before he and Jerry returned to Washington, D.C., in December 1927, when he accepted another position with the *Washington Daily News*.[165]

In 1928, Pyle began writing a feature article series on aviation, a new and exciting mode of travel. The feature became one of the first series of articles in the country devoted to the growing aviation industry. Pyle loved interviewing the pilots and capturing their courageous stories of flying planes. He met and became friends with many of those daring pilots, including Amelia Earhart.[166]

Pyle returned to the open road in 1935 when he became a roving columnist for Scripps-Howard, which owned the *Washington Daily News* and twenty-four other newspapers. For the next seven years, he submitted articles on his travel experiences throughout the United States and abroad. The articles appeared in Scripps-Howard newspapers six days a week. Using the moniker "Hoosier Vagabond," Pyle wrote about interesting people he had met and fascinating places he had seen throughout his travels. Readers loved his articles. His travel stories helped to distract the public from the gloom of the Depression and worsening news overseas as Germany and Japan began invading other countries.[167]

While passing through the Southwest, Pyle and Jerry fell in love with New Mexico and, in the summer of 1940, built their only home in Albuquerque.[168] But Pyle was never there for very long. The open road always beckoned to him.

A trip to England in December 1940 changed the course of Pyle's life and profession as a writer. England, by then, had been at war with Germany since 1939 and was getting pummeled with aerial bombs, courtesy of the German Luftwaffe. Pyle, who had turned forty, felt compelled to personally experience the war in England. He asked permission from Scripps-Howard to visit London and report on the devastation and how the British people were holding up.[169] That experience changed his life and his writing and took him down a road that would eventually end his life.

Pyle arrived in London on December 9. Within a few days, he experienced firsthand the devastation from German planes as he watched from his hotel rooftop the bombs that were dropped on buildings all around him. Although frightened by the danger, he was also mesmerized by the sights and sounds of the explosions. He was soon reporting on those experiences and interviewing British citizens who were enduring the bombings. Pyle sent his stories across the Atlantic for publication in American newspapers. They were an immediate hit with the public, which was yearning for up close and personal eyewitness accounts of what was happening in London.[170]

Pyle returned home in March 1941 when he learned that his mother had died. Following a leave of absence, Pyle returned to work and contemplated traveling to Asia and writing about the Orient.[171] The Japanese attack at Pearl Harbor on December 7, 1941, ended those plans and set in motion new ones.

Pyle returned to England in June 1942 to report on U.S. soldiers who had begun arriving in Europe for a planned invasion of German-occupied

France. Leaning on his past experiences with interviewing common people during his travels throughout the United States, he quickly developed a rapport with the servicemen whom he visited with and interviewed. He sent stories about their training across the ocean to an American public hungry to hear how their sons were doing overseas.[172]

While in England, Pyle became an official war correspondent, writing for Scripps-Howard. He arrived in North Africa in November 1942 to cover the stories of the American forces involved in the invasion, codenamed Operation Torch.[173]

Writing from Africa, he quickly developed the pattern of focusing on the common enlisted soldiers. He wasn't captivated by the strategy of combat or the perspective of high-ranking officers; he was interested in the lowly soldiers who were tasked with fighting and winning the battles. As it turned out, the American public was just as interested in them as Pyle, who was quickly becoming a favorite war correspondent back home.

Following the successful Allied invasion on Sicily in late June 1943, Pyle traveled home for rest and a reunion with Jerry. He returned to Italy in late 1943 and joined the Allied forces engaged in combat on mainland Italy.[174]

By mid-April 1944, Pyle had gone back to England to cover the Allied invasion into Northern France, codenamed Operation Overlord. On May 31, he boarded LST 353 (a Landing Ship, Tank) that soon crossed the English Channel toward Omaha Beach. He stepped onto that beach on June 7 (D-Day +1) and wrote of the battle's detritus he observed there.[175] Pyle followed the Allied army through Normandy for the next ten weeks as it battled and slowly pushed back the German forces. He was present for the liberation of Paris in late August 1944.[176]

Exhausted from almost a year on the front lines, Pyle returned home to New Mexico in early fall. He hoped that a restful break from combat would renew his energy so that he could travel to the Pacific Theater and cover the war being fought by navy, marine and army forces engaged in island-hopping campaigns as they closed in on Japan.[177] By late December, Pyle was heading to the Pacific Theater. After stops on Okinawa and Saipan and several weeks with the navy on board some ships, he came ashore on the island of Ie Shima on April 17, 1945.

The next day, April 18, he was riding in a jeep when it came under enemy fire. The men jumped out of the jeep and sought cover in nearby ditches. Pyle raised his head to see if the other men on the jeep were hurt. A concealed Japanese machine gunner had him in his crosshairs and fired. Pyle, who was forty-four years old, was killed instantly.[178]

Ernie Pyle works on an article while visiting the Anzio Beachhead, March 18, 1944. *Ernie Pyle World War II Museum.*

News of his death traveled quickly. Pyle's wife and the whole nation grieved deeply for their favorite wartime correspondent. Shortly after his death, some soldiers put up a makeshift sign on Ie Shima that read, "At this spot the 77th Infantry Division Lost a Buddy. Ernie Pyle."

Pyle was initially buried on the island of Ie Shima next to other soldiers. In 1949, his body was moved to the National Memorial Cemetery of the Pacific, Punchbowl Crater, Oahu, Hawaii, where it remains today.[179]

His stories of those who fought the war remain popular, even eighty years later. Pyle had a magical way of relating to and writing about his subjects. First earning their trust and their friendship with his non-assuming, down-to-earth ways, he expertly captured their feelings, their fears and their feats in his columns. And sometimes he captured their deaths.

He spent time with soldiers, airmen, sailors and marines, but he preferred the common infantryman in the army. He bonded with them by sharing their foxholes, eating their rations, wallowing in their mud, washing from their helmets, sleeping on their ground, smoking their cigarettes and

Ernie Pyle statue, Indiana University. *Ronald May.*

listening to their concerns and heartaches for loved ones back home. But most of all, he won hearts by sharing in their danger. Unlike many correspondents at the time, Pyle didn't grab a few quotes from the boys in foxholes and then retreat to the safety of the rear echelon. He stayed with front-line units and experienced the tedious boredom punctuated by the terror-filled moments of combat. And through it all, he captured the stories of those who faced the danger and ultimately defeated the enemy. By the end of his career, his articles were appearing in four hundred daily and three hundred weekly newspapers, making him the most well-known and widely read correspondent in World War II.[180]

Pyle's articles earned him a Pulitzer Prize in 1944, and a movie about him and the men he served with in North Africa was released in 1945, just a few months after his death. *Ernie Pyle's Story of G.I. Joe* was a hit with audiences and was nominated for four Academy Awards.

In 1995, fifty years after his death, the Ernie Pyle World War II Museum opened in Dana. The museum creatively presents many of his wartime stories through print and dioramic exhibits. The exhibits fill two World War II–era Quonset huts next to the home where he was born. Each diorama creates a scene from a popular Pyle dispatch. Visitors have the option of reading his column or picking up a phone receiver and listening to an excerpt of the column. Seeing the dioramas while reading the articles associated with them transports the visitor to the people and places found in Pyle's writing. Especially moving is the diorama inside the Waskow Theater showing a soldier, kneeling down, paying his respects to his dead captain. Through a combination of video clips and lights on two mannequins, it re-creates the scene of Pyle's most evocative and well-known article on the death of Captain Waskow.

In addition to artifacts, photos and a small gift shop, there are also small theaters that show archival video clips of Pyle's life and his work as a correspondent. There is a wall dedicated to the service of more than three hundred Helt Township veterans in the gift shop. Visitors can learn about each of their service stories by using the kiosk beside the wall.

The museum is well worth a visit. It is open on weekends from May to Veterans Day and is maintained by the Friends of Ernie Pyle, a nonprofit organization. For more information, visit www.erniepyle.org.

A few miles east of Dana, on the stretch of Highway 36 designated the Ernie Pyle Memorial Highway, is the Ernie Pyle Rest Park, which includes a concrete pyramid marker like the one erected on the island of Ie Shima, commemorating his death.

Dana isn't the only town in Indiana to preserve Pyle's service. In 2014, Indiana University in Bloomington dedicated a statue of Pyle working as a war correspondent. Sitting on a crate at his field desk, Pyle is typing an article on his portable typewriter. The statue is in front of the Media School at Franklin Hall, just inside the historic Sample Gate, on the campus of Indiana University, Pyle's alma mater.[181]

Inside the Media School, on the lower level, is a hallway dedicated to Pyle's work as a correspondent. Display cases contain items belonging to Pyle. Photos of him adorn the walls alongside the displays.

The Hoosier native, who traded Indiana farm work for a lifetime of world travel and wartime service, will be fondly remembered and honored in his home state for generations to come, thanks in part to the Ernie Pyle World War II Museum and Indiana University.[182]

For more information, visit https://erniepyle.org.

10

WORLD WAR II MEMORIAL
OF PUTNAM COUNTY

Most war memorials that incorporate military equipment or artifacts use U.S. or Allied pieces. Tanks and artillery are popular choices. When Putnam County, Indiana, created its memorial for World War II veterans, it took a completely different approach. It used a German V-1 Flying Buzz Bomb.

Located on the southwest corner of the Putnam County Courthouse in Greencastle, the plane-shaped bomb looks like an antiquated missile system ready to launch an attack from the air.

Built by Germany, it was used in World War II against the Allies. German scientists working for the Luftwaffe first designed it in 1939 as one of the earliest auto-guided missile systems. It could be launched on the ground from an elevated track or secured to the underside of a plane and dropped from the air. Hitler began using it in 1944 against England as a terror bomb.[183] And it readily produced the desired effect.

Germany called it the *Vergeltungswaffe* ("Vengeance Weapon," hence the abbreviation V-1). The Allies called it the "Buzz Bomb" for the buzzing sound that it made in flight. The British labeled it the "Doodlebug."[184] Regardless of what name was used, it packed a punch.

The V-1 was twenty-seven feet long, seventeen feet wide and almost five feet tall. It weighed 4,740 pounds, which included its 2,000-pound warhead. It could travel distances of up to 160 miles at a speed of 400 miles per hour and at an altitude between two thousand and three thousand feet. Germany produced thirty thousand of them.[185]

V-1 Buzz Bomb, Putnam County War Memorial. *Ronald May.*

That Hitler was using the pilotless missiles at all was evidence of his diminishing fleet of planes and pilots in the Luftwaffe. In 1940, the German Luftwaffe began its bombing blitz over London. While the bombs dropped from German planes resulted in much destruction of property and considerable loss of life, the cost in loss of Nazi planes and pilots proved to be too high for the Germans to sustain the air attacks. Thanks to the great aerial defense of England by British Spitfires and other planes, the Luftwaffe stopped its manned aerial attacks in May 1941.

Three years later, Germany resumed its aerial bombing over London on June 13, 1944, this time using its pilotless V-1. Largely a response to the Allied landing at Normandy, the V-1s were launched from ground facilities along the Pas-de-Calais on the French coast. From June through October that year, more than 9,500 V-1 missiles were fired at southeast England. At times, more than 100 of them were launched in one day.[186]

Upon impact, the V-1 unleashed its vengeance. Of the almost 10,000 buzz bombs that were fired at England, 2,419 hit targets in and near London, killing 6,184 Britons and injuring 17,981. The explosions also caused significant damage to buildings and property.[187]

The British Royal Air Force and ground antiaircraft artillery quickly grew in their capability of shooting down the terror weapon. They brought down more than four thousand of the V-1s before they could detonate. Sadly, there were still a large number that reached their target and caused terror and destruction.[188]

John (Jack) Welsh observed several V-1s in flight over England while serving in the navy on an LCI (Landing Craft Infantry). The Greencastle, Indiana native enlisted in the navy in February 1942. He became an engineering officer assigned to LCI(L) 517, one of the navy's many Landing Craft Infantry (Large) vessels that transported troops to the shore. Welsh's ship arrived on the English coast in March 1944 to participate in training exercises for the upcoming invasion at Normandy. It was from there that he saw the buzz bombs flying overhead.[189] "As we went from port to port along England's southern coast, we frequently heard and then saw the German V-1 and V-2 jet-propelled bombs," he recalled in an unpublished memoir he wrote for his family in 2004.

> The V-1 bombs sounded like outboard motors as they flew along. They were only about five hundred to one thousand-feet high, so they were very visible from the ship and from the countryside. As long as the bombs kept going, we knew we were safe. However, when the engine stopped, the bomb, which looked like a small plane, went down and exploded. I am sure that they did quite a lot of damage, and killed many people, but we usually did not see the newspapers, so we did not know how many people were killed or how much damage was done. Thankfully, none of them dropped on us.[190]

The use of the bombs on England progressively lessened after the Allied invasion of Normandy as air and ground forces in France located and disarmed them. By October 1944, the Allies had captured or destroyed most of the V-1 launching sites in coastal France, bringing an end to their "vengeance" on London.[191]

After attacking London became untenable, the retreating Germans directed their V-1 attacks on the port at Antwerp, Belgium, where most of the Allied supplies arrived from the United States. From October 1944 to March 1945, the German Luftwaffe launched 2,448 V-1s toward Antwerp. Improved antiaircraft measures resulted in only 211 of the bombs successfully hitting their intended targets.[192] The use of the V-1 continued until one month before Germany surrendered in May 1945.[193]

Jack Welsh sitting on an LCI underway. *Jack Welsh family.*

Three years later, one of those surviving V-1 bombs arrived in Greencastle, Indiana, through the efforts of local resident Frank Durham, a naval reservist. In 1947, during his two weeks of annual training for explosive ordnance demolition at Fort Stumpneck, Maryland, he learned that a Buzz Bomb in U.S. possession was about to be destroyed due to lack of storage space. Thinking that the bomb would make a great exhibit back in his hometown, he inquired about taking possession of it. He was told by his commanding officer that it would probably take an act of Congress to receive permission. Undeterred, Durham began the process of petitioning Congress through Indiana senator William Jenner. By February 1948, Congress had approved his request for the bomb to be transferred to the Veterans of Foreign Wars (VFW) Post 1550 in Greencastle, which offered its assistance with the effort to display it as a veterans memorial.[194]

The project received overwhelming community approval and financial support by businesses and individuals. The memorial was dedicated on November 11, 1948, with a crowd of more than five thousand attending and Rear Admiral A.G. Noble, chief of the Bureau of Ordnance, serving as the guest speaker.[195]

The V-1 rests on a large limestone base that is in the shape of a *V*. The base was designed by DePauw University student Art Perry. The limestone for the base was graciously donated by former Indiana state senator William B. Hoadley of Bloomington (1928–32, 1952–56), who was part owner of the Indiana Limestone Company in Bloomington. Hughes lost his only son, Staff Sergeant William Hughes Hoadley, age twenty, in October 1944, during combat in Luxembourg. The younger Hughes was a graduate of Bloomington High School and had completed three years of studies at Indiana University before enlisting in the army in May 1943.[196]

On the ground next to the limestone base is a marker that provides a brief description of the Buzz Bomb and states, "It is intended as a memorial to the men of Putnam County who lost their lives in World War II."

As impressive as the V-1 and limestone base are, the most important feature of the memorial is a bronze plaque placed into a recessed area at the bottom of the base. The top of the plaque has an eagle with extended wings. Underneath the eagle are the words "Dedicated to All Who Served and Died in World War II." The names of the seventy-three men from Putnam County who were killed in action are listed as "Our Hallowed Dead" and are memorialized for future generations. The plaque notes that the memorial is presented by the citizens of Putnam County.

It might seem peculiar at first for the citizens of Putnam County to have a German weapon of vengeance on display at their courthouse—even more so to use it as a memorial for the men from their county who died in that war. However, the peculiarity of the V-1's presence is ingenious. While it is a weapon the Germans used against the Allies, it is a weapon that ultimately, like every German weapon, was silenced because of the Allied air attacks and infantry advance that eventually killed or chased away the men needed to launch the V-1.[197]

In retrospect, the limestone *V* platform of the memorial represents the first letter for "Victory" over Germany. Putnam County pays tribute to its husbands, sons, brothers and friends who secured that victory with their lives.[198]

11

WORLD WAR II MEMORIAL PARK

Many memorials are located on main streets, town squares or city parks. The town leaders of Avon, a western suburb of Indianapolis, chose to place their memorial in a residential area next to an elementary school.

You know you are getting close to the Avon World War II Memorial Park when you drive around the cul-de-sac at Dan Jones Road and County Road 100 South and see the banners of local World War II service members hanging from poles around the circle. The memorial park comes into view on the north side of 100 South as soon as you proceed west from the intersection.

Dedicated on May 4, 2013, the one-acre park pays tribute to the men and women who served during World War II.[199]

The memorial, planned by the Avon World War II Memorial Park Committee and funded by the Avon Parks Foundation, is built on a concrete circle that has a large blue service star in the middle.[200] There are four benches on the south perimeter of the memorial. Each bench bears the title for one of our nation's virtues: Peace, Freedom, Dignity and Justice.

Dominating the north side of the memorial are large flagpoles from which our National Ensign and five service branch flags fly: U.S. Army, Navy, Air Force, Marines and Coast Guard. Six small granite service monuments with laurel wreaths of victory rest on the ground in front of the flagpoles.

The central feature of the memorial is a six-foot bronze statue of a World War II soldier in a field uniform, helmet resting on his head, a rifle slung on his right shoulder. He stands on a granite pyramid pillar in a posture of

Avon World War II Memorial Park. *Ronald May.*

vigilance and duty. The soldier's face bears the likeness of local war hero Clyde C. (Chet) Wright.

Born in 1918, Wright grew up on the west side of Indianapolis and was a 1938 graduate of Ben Davis High School. In 1940, he enlisted in the Indiana National Guard. After completing his basic training at Camp Shelby, Mississippi, he was assigned to the 139th Field Artillery Battalion in the 38th Division. He became a warrant officer in 1942. His division was sent in 1943 to the Pacific Theater, where Wright spent the next three years. His artillery battalion provided fire support for combat operations in New Guinea, the Philippines and Luzon.[201]

During an interview for the Library of Congress Veterans History Project on May 8, 2007, Wright recalled his World War II service. "We talk about D-Day in Europe when they made a big landing; we had D-Days just about every week, going somewhere on a small boat."[202] He spoke of his unit's proudest moment following their landing at Luzon: "The 38th Infantry Division—and I was part of it—we retook the Bataan Peninsula [Island of Luzon in the Philippines]. It took us quite a while. They put up a big sign—General MacArthur did—he had a sign erected, 'You are entering the Bataan Peninsula, courtesy of the 38th Infantry Division.' We were known as the 'Avengers of Bataan.'"[203]

Chester Wright service photo. *Wright family.*

On one occasion, their artillery support included firing in the direction of one of their sister battalions. Wright explained during the interview that the Japanese had overrun the position of the 163rd field artillery battalion. "They got in their foxholes, and they called in their coordinates where they were and said fire in our direction," he recalled. The artillery barrage worked, and the enemy scattered.[204]

Wright's career didn't end with his World War II service. After returning home following his discharge in 1946, he received a call asking him to join the Indiana Army National Guard, where he served until 1978, rising to the rank of a brigadier general. He came out of retirement in 1981 and served for the next five years as the commanding general for the Indiana National Guard. Wright retired the second time, and for good, in 1986, having completed forty-five years of military service.[205]

When the town of Avon decided to create a World War II Memorial in 2009, organizers asked Wright to serve on the committee. He didn't realize at the time that native Hoosier and nationally renowned sculptor Bill Wolfe, commissioned to create the bronze statue, was using a photo of Wright from his World War II service for the likeness of the soldier's face.[206]

Wolfe recalled the groundbreaking ceremony on June 7, 2012, attended by more than three hundred people: "The town of Avon invited him [Wright] to the future site of the monument. I had a poster made that included an image of General Wright and the clay model of the future statue. He was in his nineties and used a walker, and I asked him to step up to the easel to unveil the featured person for the monument. The general was surprised, honored and proud when he found out he was going to be the focus of the future monument to the veterans. He was a sweet and well-liked man with so much character in his face. It was a pleasure for me to meet such an honorable man and to create the bronze statue of him."[207]

The four-sided granite pyramid on which the soldier with Wright's image stands is in the middle of the large blue service star. On one side of the pyramid is an engraved quote from President Harry Truman: "Our debt to the heroic men and valiant women in the service of our country can never be repaid. They have earned our undying gratitude. America will never forget their sacrifices. Because of these sacrifices, the dawn of justice and freedom throughout the world will slowly cast its gleam across the horizon."[208]

Another side of the pyramid quotes President Dwight D. Eisenhower: "We must be ready to dare all for our country. For history does not long entrust the care of freedom to the weak or the timid. We must acquire proficiency in defense and display stamina in purpose. We must be willing, individually and as a nation, to accept whatever sacrifices may be required of us. A people that values its privileges above its principles soon loses both."[209]

A bronze plaque summarizing Wright's military career is affixed to a large rock on the west side of the memorial. The summary ends with these words: "On behalf of a grateful nation and the citizens of Avon, Indiana, we are honored to recognize General Clyde C. 'Chet' Wright as a citizen-soldier who represents the character and spirit of our Greatest Generation."[210]

Wright shared his reaction to the memorial in a video clip following the dedication ceremony on May 4, 2013. "I think it is outstanding. I think it shows what a small town can do to keep our freedom that we have endured for so many years. I think the importance is to let people know what we have so near to our hearts and try to endure to keep it going."[211]

The location of the memorial next to Pine Tree Elementary School in Avon ensures that local students from the next generation remember those 16 million men and women who, like Mr. Wright, helped protect the freedom that remains so "near to our hearts."

12

INDIANA WAR MEMORIAL
AND MUSEUM

Throughout the Hoosier heartland, there are memorials, museums and monuments that commemorate those who fought in World Wars I and II. The crown jewel of them all is the Indiana War Memorial in Indianapolis. Located a few blocks north of the city center, the memorial anchors the south terminus of the Veteran's Memorial Plaza and the American Legion Mall, two grassy areas that extend three blocks north.

Dressed in Indiana limestone and adorned with a pyramid crown, the memorial's large cube structure rises 210 feet from the ground.[212] Its Neoclassical architecture is reminiscent of ancient Greece, with its six Ionic columns reaching high from the top of each side of the building.[213]

Although originally built to honor the 150,000-plus World War I veterans from Indiana who served in that war, the memorial was rededicated in 1966, with some controversy, to also commemorate the 400,000 Hoosier veterans who fought in World War II and the 143,000 Hoosiers who served in the Korean Conflict.[214]

Begun in 1926, the cornerstone for the building was laid on July 4, 1927, by General John P. ("Blackjack") Pershing, the commander of the American Expeditionary Forces during World War I. The memorial was completed and dedicated in 1933.[215]

The Pershing Auditorium is the central and largest room on the main floor of the building. The ornate space, which includes five hundred seats and a balcony, is trimmed in American red marble and treated with special acoustical tiles. Public and private events are held there throughout the year.[216]

Indiana War Memorial, southeast side. *Ronald May.*

On the east and west sides of the memorial's main floor are two large meeting rooms that accommodate up to seventy-five people. Both rooms are named after famous World War II military leaders with Indiana roots: Admiral Raymond Spruance, commander of naval forces in the Pacific, who grew up in Indianapolis, and Marine Corps general David Shoup, who led marine forces in the Pacific and later became the commandant of the Marine Corps. He grew up in Covington, Indiana.

Above the auditorium, on the top level, is the magnificent Shrine Room, which is accessed by elevator or by long stairwells on either side of the auditorium. If one's health and fitness level allow, it is preferable to climb the stairs to see the many thousand names listed in alphabetical order in picture frames on either side of the stairway. These are the names of 150,000 Hoosiers who participated in World War I, as well as the thousands who were killed or declared missing in action from World War II, Korea and Vietnam.[217] The seemingly endless display of names provides a sobering scope to the sheer volume of young Hoosiers who served, many of whom suffered the ultimate sacrifice in our nation's service.

A magnificent Shrine Room rewards the visitor who has climbed the stairwell or ridden the elevator to the top of the memorial. Walking into the space, the visitor immediately senses that he or she has entered a holy realm.

The 60-square-foot room has a ceiling that rises 110 feet to the underside of the pyramid roof.[218] Looking up to the peak of the pyramid, myriad bright-blue lights—like stars from the heavens—twinkle in the darkness around a large golden star: the Star of Destiny, made of Swedish crystal, which beams brightly and symbolizes the light that guides the nation.[219] Near the top of each wall are several rows of vertical stained-glass windows that are colored blue and let in a little natural daylight to an otherwise darker and more somber space. Twenty-four columns made from Vermont red marble forty feet high stand guard over the sacred space—six on each side of the room. Their blood-red color symbolizes the blood sacrificed in service to the nation.[220]

The central feature of the room is a massive American flag that hangs down beneath the Star of Destiny in stately grandeur. Beneath the flag, on a black marble platform, is the Altar of Consecration, made from black and reddish-brown marble, which bears witness to the fallen heroes who have fought under the flag.

The whole room has a grandeur that evokes awe. It was designed by the architect to inspire the gazer to the high call of patriotism and citizenship, while serving as a reminder for those who have fought and died in preserving our nation's freedom.[221]

While the Shrine Room inspires the visitor, the free museum at the lowest level of the building informs and educates those who take the time to walk through it. The many fine exhibits chronologically showcase the involvement of Indiana veterans in all our nation's wars, beginning with the Revolutionary War and extending to the more recent War on Terrorism.

U.S. flag hanging from the Shrine Room. *Ronald May.*

Governor Edgar Whitcomb display. *Ronald May.*

The museum is easily one of the best in the Midwest. It is well worth the time to walk through it!

There is much to see and learn in the World War II gallery. It includes displays of uniforms, weapons, photos, newspaper headlines, paintings and documents, as well as other interesting artifacts.

One exhibit memorializes the service of U.S. Army Air Corps navigator Edgar Whitcomb, who later became Indiana's forty-third governor. The items in the corner exhibit include a painted portrait with a summary of his military service, a photo of him with General James Doolittle, the two books he wrote of his war service and the sextant he used in his navigation while serving on a B-17.

Whitcomb's daring service story is also summarized in a digitized version of the Golden Book in the Memorial Room of the Indiana Memorial Union at Indiana University, Whitcomb's alma mater:[222]

> *Whitcomb was born in Hayden, Indiana, in 1917. He came to Indiana University in 1939 intending to study law. With the outbreak of World War II, he left the university to serve in the Army Air Corps, becoming a navigator on B-17 bombers. He arrived in the Philippines just a few weeks before the Japanese began their conquest. When Whitcomb's base was overrun by the Japanese, he and other Americans were driven into the Bataan Peninsula. When the remaining American forces surrendered, Whitcomb was not one of them.*

Whitcomb and two others escaped from Bataan in a rowboat and went to Corregidor. When Corregidor fell to the Japanese, again Whitcomb was one of several to escape being taken prisoner. This time he did so by swimming for eight hours across the sea to get back to the mainland. Then he began his journey of eluding Japanese forces as he and a small group made their way across the country, got a small sailboat to make it to China, and were eventually captured by the Japanese. Beaten and tortured but believed to be a civilian, Whitcomb was sent to China and then India before being repatriated. He arrived back in the United States in December of 1943. He eventually returned to the Philippines as part of the American invasion force.

After the war, Whitcomb served in the Army Reserves until 1977 when he retired as a colonel. Whitcomb had returned to IU and graduated from the Law School in 1950, and the same year was elected to his first political office as a member of the Indiana State Senate. He later became Indiana Secretary of State and was elected the forty-third Governor of the State of Indiana in 1968.

After his time in public office, Whitcomb returned to his law practice, retiring in 1985, and took up sailing as his hobby. In 1995, he sailed around the world.[223]

In 1958, Whitcomb published his first book about his war service and daring escape from the Japanese, *Escape from Corregidor*.[224] Adventurous and productive even in his later years, he remained in Indiana the rest of his life and died at the age of ninety-eight in 2016. Two years before his death, a monument to him was dedicated in his hometown of Hayden.[225]

Just beyond the Whitcomb exhibit in the War Memorial Museum is a room that showcases the contributions of many of the companies throughout Indiana that made products for the war effort. Divided into regions of the state, information boards identify the companies and what they produced during the war. There are also displays of some of those products.

After finishing the tour of the museum and climbing the stairs back to the main level, visitors will walk past the USS *Indianapolis* Gallery. Here there are many items related to the heavy cruiser that was sunk at the end of the war: a model of the ship; the ship's bell; painted portraits by local Indiana artist Jack Gromosiak, who captured different scenes from the sinking of the USS *Indianapolis* with his paintbrush; a large map showing the routes of the ship's many missions in the Pacific Theater; display cases with uniforms and photos of sailors who served on the ship; and storyboards that tell the ship's service history and the rescue of the survivors. A re-created ship's radio room, modeled after the one in the USS *Indianapolis*, can also be visited. It is to the right of the exit doors off the main lobby.

Preparing to exit the memorial, visitors will notice the large bronze marker paying tribute to Hoosiers throughout our nation's wars who have been awarded the Medal of Honor for their acts of gallantry.

Upon exiting the memorial, visitors will be treated to a great view of the Veterans Memorial Plaza and American Legion Mall stretching out for three city blocks. The grassy area has additional monuments. It also features memorials for World War II, Korea and Vietnam.

The Indiana War Memorial building, which is open Wednesdays through Sundays 9:00 a.m. to 5:00 p.m. and is free to the public, is located on Michigan Avenue between Pennsylvania and Meridian Streets in downtown Indianapolis. It is managed by the Indiana War Memorial Commission.[226]

For more information, visit https://www.in.gov/iwm/indiana-war-memorial-museum.

13

WORLD WAR II MEMORIAL

Dear Mom and Dad. This is a letter that I hope need not be delivered, for that would mean that I am considered missing or killed in action.[227]

Those are the opening words to a letter that Vernon C. Buchanan of Indianapolis wrote to his parents in late 1944. He hoped that it would not be mailed from the Philippines, where he was serving in the U.S. Army Air Forces. Tragically, the letter was mailed to his parents in early 1945, notifying them of their son's death on January 9, 1945.[228] A second lieutenant, he was a B-25 bomber pilot serving in the Pacific with the 500th Bomb Squadron, 345th Bomb Group. He went missing on January 9 following a mission and was never found.[229]

Buchanan's letter has been made public and read by thousands of people because his words have been inscribed on the World War II Memorial in downtown Indianapolis.

The memorial was a long time in coming. In the decades after the war, there were attempts to introduce legislation for the building of a memorial in Indianapolis. But nothing found traction until the legislative director for Amvets, Joseph Riley, a navy veteran who served in the mid-1950s, personally took initiative. In 1997, he approached Representative B. Patrick Bauer, chairman of the Indiana House Ways and Means Committee, and boldly asked for $350,000 for the building of a memorial. This time, the request for funding was granted.[230] The project began on Veterans Day 1997 and cost $425,000 to build.[231] The remaining $75,000 was paid for by private donations.[232]

World War II Memorial interior. "In Memory of Those Who Served." *Ronald May*.

Just six months later, the memorial was dedicated on May 22, 1998. Retired senator Bob Dole, the national face of World War II veterans at that time, served as guest speaker.[233] Indiana governor Frank O'Bannon also made remarks. Popular television journalist Tom Brokaw, who published his book *The Greatest Generation* that same year, was also on hand. A crowd of one thousand gathered for the dedication on a rainy day.[234]

The World War II Memorial came two years after the city dedicated the Korean and Vietnam Memorials in 1996 on the west and east sides of the American Legion mall.

Designed by Fort Wayne architect Patrick Brunner, the memorial consists of a half-cylinder structure constructed of polished granite and limestone trim. Differing slightly from the Vietnam and Korean Memorials partial-cylinder designs, the World War II Memorial is in the shape of a half circle. The nine-feet, two-inch radius is intentionally larger than the Vietnam and Korean Memorials, to signify the larger scale of that war and the greater numbers of those killed in action.[235]

Nationally, almost 500,000 Americans were killed during World War II. The Hoosier portion of that grim figure is almost 12,000. Another 17,000 survived but came home to Indiana with significant wounds.[236]

The convex side of the memorial faces east toward Pennsylvania Street and includes a narrative of U.S. involvement in the war. Inside the engraved borders of Indiana are the number of Hoosiers who served in the war (395,982), as well as those injured and lost in the war. The convex side also

World War II Memorial exterior, Indianapolis. *Ronald May.*

identifies the nine Hoosier Medal of Honor recipients, along with Hoosier military units that received distinguished recognition. At the bottom of the wall is a world map showing the Allied and Axis countries, along with the Axis conquests by December 1941.

On the concave side, facing west toward the plaza, are excerpts from letters home written by Hoosier veterans who fought in World War II. A cylindrical column, unique to this memorial, stands in front of the half-circle monument. It lists, in order of sequence, the campaigns and major operations of the war and their respective dates.

Buchannan's is not the only letter to appear on the wall. William Rudy's letter to his parents is inscribed as well. He was luckier than Buchanan—he survived the war, but he came home missing part of his left leg.

Rudy, also from Indianapolis, was born in 1922 and graduated from Shortridge High School. He completed two years at Indiana University before enlisting in Army Air Force Cadet Training. He reported for duty in early 1943.[237] Following his flight training, he was assigned as a navigator on a B-24 Liberator and deployed to Italy in July 1944. His plane was shot down by flak over Skoplje, Yugoslavia, on August 17 while returning from a mission to bomb the oil fields in Ploesti, Romania. It was his eighth mission.[238]

He and his crew bailed out of the bomber as it was going down. Upon reaching the ground, Rudy was captured by some Bulgarian soldiers, one of whom shot him in the left leg, just below his calf. A few weeks later, his infected lower leg was amputated in a Yugoslavian hospital.[239] He spent the next few months being moved from place to place until finally landing at Stalag XVIII-A, a German POW camp in southern Austria, where he remained until his liberation by the British on May 9, 1945, the day after Germany surrendered.[240] Having endured an amputation and nine months of captivity, he was finally sent home.[241]

It was in February 1945, six months into his captivity, that Rudy sent a letter to his folks back home in Indianapolis informing them of his condition and expressing his gratitude for being alive. His words are found on the memorial wall:

William Rudy. *Rudy family.*

> *Dear Folks, I am very comfortable situated in a prison hospital in Germany and very thankful to be alive. You may as well know that my left foot and part of my leg have been amputated. The doctors don't have much hope of saving my knee which was left stiff as the result of the operation. All amputation cases are eligible for automatic repatriation, so I think the doctors are going to delay a second amputation until the physicians in America have a chance to look at it. But don't get too impatient about this repatriation because it may take six months to a year. Losing my leg seemed pretty awful to me at first, but I have grown used to it now and realize how lucky I am not to be dead.*
>
> *Love, Bill. (William B. Rudy, Indianapolis. Stalag XVIII, February 1945)*[242]

The other inscriptions on the wall include an excerpt from President Roosevelt's December 8, 1941 address to Congress, a quote from President Truman lauding the spirit of liberty on September 1, 1945, following the surrender of Japan, a portion of Ernie Pyle's "A Last Word" column from August 1944 and personal letters home from a soldier and a sailor, as well as a letter by a woman in Indianapolis sharing her thoughts following the announcement of the D-Day invasion in France.

While the letters are sobering reminders of the tragic losses suffered in World War II, they are also inspirational testimonies in their stated devotion to the war's cause. The remainder of Buchanan's letter, also on the memorial, speaks to his willingness to die that others might live:

Please don't think that you have lost everything in losing your son. Remember that I volunteered for this and knew what it might lead to. I have spent some of my happiest moments in the A.A.F. I feel I have done something to be proud of, something perhaps that will aid America to remain "the land of the free, the home of the brave." If my death helps end this war one minute sooner, I consider it worthwhile…

Eternally your son,

Vernon (Vernon C. Buchanan, Indianapolis, Killed in Action, Philippines, 1944)[243]

There is another theme to one of the memorial letters, that of yearning to maintain a connection to the Indiana soil for those who fought on foreign ground so far away. A moving poem entitled "Elegy," written by James McGregor of Munster, Indiana, appears on the bottom center of the interior memorial wall.

McGregor joined the army in 1942. He was serving on the Pacific Island of Biak, northwest of New Guinea, in 1944 when he penned the poem. Nobody knew anything about the poem until his widow, Charlotte, came across it after his death in 1995. Having read about the plans to build a World War II memorial in Indianapolis, she sent a copy of the poem to the memorial committee. The committee members decided to include his poem on the monument. His stirring words are now read by everyone who visits the memorial:[244]

"Elegy"

There's a bit of Indiana in the sighing of the breeze.
There's a hint of Indiana in the rustling of the trees.
And the Jungle's myriad whisperings are sibilantly clear.
("They are having injun summer,"
just ten thousand miles from here.)
There's a part of Indiana in the blazing tropic moon.
There's a trace of Indiana in the shimmering lagoon.
And a message in the tramping of a sentry very near:
("Oh, the frost is on the punkin,"
just ten thousand miles from here.)
There's a share of Indiana in the crosses by the palms,

There's a touch of Indiana in the South Pacific Calms.
And the murmur of the breakers brings me desolating cheer
("Oh, the corn is heavy on the stalk,"
just ten thousand miles from here.)
There's a piece of Indiana where the sand is stained with red:
There's a lot of Indiana where the Hoosier lays his head.
And I seem to hear him saying as I stand beside his Bier:
("Let me sleep once more beneath the Sky,"
ten thousand miles from here.)[245]

Thanks to McGregor's poem, those who never returned to the Indiana soil and the people they loved and longed for are still linked to their home state in the hearts and minds of visitors who stop to read and reflect.

14

NATIONAL MEDAL OF HONOR MEMORIAL

On a warm and bright sunny afternoon on May 28, 1999, a new memorial was unveiled along the north bank of the Indiana Central Canal, just west of downtown Indianapolis. Close to ten thousand people crowded along the canal to honor the nearly one hundred special guests who had come from different parts of the country to be honored and to help dedicate the memorial.[246] The special guests, wearing their distinctive five-point gold stars hanging from pale-blue silk ribbons around their necks, were the living recipients of the nation's highest military award, the Congressional Medal of Honor.

The memorial was the brainchild of John Hodowal, chairman of the Indianapolis Power and Light Company (IPALCO). In June 1998, he and his wife, Caroline, were moved by a story they read in the *New York Times* about the living Medal of Honor recipients attending their annual convention and sharing their challenges with combat memories and getting back to normal life at home. Inspired by the story, which brought them both to tears, they decided to help create a memorial in Indianapolis to honor all recipients of our nation's highest military medal.[247]

Groundbreaking for the memorial was held in November 1998, and construction began in January 1999.[248] The two living Medal of Honor recipients with Indiana roots, Melvin Biddle and Sammy L. Davis, were invited to help pour the first load of cement and offer remarks.[249]

National Medal of Honor Memorial. *Ronald May.*

Eric Fulford and Ann Reed, a husband-and-wife landscape architect duo in Indianapolis, designed the monument. IPALCO provided the funding and served as sponsor for the $2.5 million project.[250]

The memorial consists of twenty-seven emerald curved glass panels standing between seven and ten feet high. The panels are anchored to concrete bases resting on Indiana limestone and secured to one another by metal braces. Each panel has two layers. The exterior layer is translucent, with decorative lines and swirls. The interior panel is clear glass. Etched on the glass panels are the names of 3,515 Medal of Honor recipients, along with their rank and the location where they rendered their valorous service.[251] The fifteen walls of panels are grouped according to war periods from the Civil War to the present.

The memorial is fittingly adjacent to the historic Military Park, which served as a mustering and training site for Union soldiers preparing to fight in the Civil War, the first conflict for which Medals of Honor were awarded.

The sunrise that peeks over the majestic downtown skyline shines brilliantly on the emerald glass memorial, as does the setting sun from the west. The sun, however, is not the only light that shines on the memorial. Motion-sensor lights are installed between the dual glass panes and light up at night as a person walks past the memorial. Audio recordings summarizing the service of the recipients play from speakers installed around the memorial. The combination of lights and sounds brings the memorial to life each evening.

For those who want to learn more about the honorees, there is a kiosk at the back of the memorial that visitors can use to search and read accounts of each recipient's service for which they received their medals.

There are 472 veterans of World War II who received the Medal of Honor, 10 of them from Indiana.[252] One name etched in the glass of the memorial's World War II section is a local hero from Indianapolis who served as an army medic.

William D. McGee was born in 1923 and graduated from Arsenal Technical High School in 1941. Enlisting in the army in December 1942, he trained as a medic at Camp Bowie in Texas and was then assigned to the Medical Detachment, K Company, 304th Infantry Regiment, 76th Infantry Division. Arriving in Europe in the spring of 1944, McGee's medical detachment was part of General George Patton's 3rd Army, which had pushed quickly across France and Belgium and was penetrating Germany.[253]

William D. McGee photo and glass etching on memorial. *Service photo in public domain; image of etching taken by author.*

On March 18, 1945, McGee's unit crossed the Moselle River with plans to advance into Mulheim, Germany. As the first wave of men left their rafts and proceeded up the river's bank, they came upon an unknown minefield that had been laid by the retreating Germans. Two men stepped on the mines and were grievously wounded.[254]

Abandoning caution, McGee disregarded his commanding officer's orders not to proceed, saying, "It is my duty to go after them." The medic bravely advanced alone across the minefield to retrieve the two men who had been injured. He reached the first one and brought him to safety. When McGee went back for the second injured man, he stepped on one of the mines and suffered fatal wounds from the blast.[255]

Other men from his unit wanted to rescue the bleeding and severely injured medic, but McGee, who was still conscious, refused aid and sternly

National Medal of Honor Memorial along downtown canal lit by lights and the moon. *Ronald May.*

pleaded for the men to stay back and not risk setting off another mine. McGee bled out and died in front of his comrades. He was twenty-two years old.[256]

His Medal of Honor citation commemorates his valor and concludes with these words: "In making the supreme sacrifice, Private McGee demonstrated a concern for the well-being of his fellow soldiers that transcended all considerations for his own safety and a gallantry in keeping with the highest traditions of the military service."[257]

Eleven months after his death, on February 23, 1946, McGee was posthumously awarded the Medal of Honor. The award, along with the Purple Heart he earned for his injuries, was presented to his widow, Ruth, at Fort Benjamin Harrison in Indianapolis.[258]

McGee is one of seventy-nine medical personnel who have received the Medal of Honor in their roles as doctors, nurses, medics and corpsmen.[259]

McGee's widow, Ruth, made her own sacrifice when she chose to have the body of her beloved William permanently buried at the American Cemetery in Luxembourg City as a visible reminder of Americans' service in Europe.[260]

The prime location of the Medal of Honor Memorial along the popular three-mile downtown canal ensures that hundreds of people will pass by each day and be reminded of the heroic sacrifices of McGee and the other 3,500 plus recipients who have received our nation's highest military award for their valorous service.[261]

15

USS *INDIANAPOLIS* MEMORIAL

O hear us when we cry to thee
For those in peril on the sea!
—refrain from "Eternal Father, Strong to Save," the Navy Hymn

It was a memorial thirty years in the making, commemorating a tragedy fifty years in the past. The USS *Indianapolis* Memorial was dedicated on August 2, 1995, along the east bank of the Indiana Central Canal in downtown Indianapolis, the namesake for the ship. The event marked the fiftieth anniversary of the heavy cruiser's sinking by a Japanese submarine at the end of World War II.

The story of the *Indianapolis* is one of the most tragic of the war. On July 26, 1945, the USS *Indianapolis* (CA-35) arrived at the Pacific Island of Tinian to drop off top-secret cargo. No one on the ship—surprisingly, not even the ship's commander, Captain Charles B. McVay III—knew the contents of that mysterious cargo.[262] Of the 1,196 men in the ship's crew, most would never know they had just delivered parts for the atomic bomb, codenamed "Little Boy," that was later assembled on Tinian and, on August 6, dropped over Hiroshima, Japan. Most of the crew never learned what they delivered because they died in the worst naval sea disaster of World War II.

Commissioned in 1932, CA-35, one of the navy's heavy cruisers, was the third ship to be named for the city of Indianapolis. It was active in Pacific Theater combat missions throughout World War II.

USS *Indianapolis* CA-35, Mare Island Naval Shipyard, July 10, 1945. *Bureau of Ships Collection, U.S. National Archives.*

The heavy cruiser's most important mission—and it would be the last one—came in the summer of 1945, when it received the top-secret cargo. On July 16, *Indianapolis* departed from Hunters Point Naval Shipyard in San Francisco and sped toward its assigned destination, the island of Tinian, reaching it ten days later, on July 26. There its top-secret cargo was unloaded.[263]

After a brief stop in Guam on July 28, the *Indianapolis* headed out to sea again for the last time. Its destination was Leyte, the largest of the Philippine Islands.[264] At 12:05 a.m. on July 30, Japanese submarine *I-58*, commanded by Mochitsura Hashimoto, spotted the *Indianapolis* and fired six torpedoes at it. Two made contact, striking the bow and amidships.[265]

Minutes later, McVay passed the order to abandon the sinking ship. Radio operators in the ship's communications room sent off hasty S.O.S. transmissions.[266] Within twelve minutes, the *Indianapolis* succumbed to its fatal injuries and descended beneath the water. Some three hundred crewmen, entombed in its entrails, went down with it to the bottom of the sea.[267] But the tragedy had just begun.

The rest of the crew, almost nine hundred men, managed to get off the ship before it sank, but many of them were injured from the ship's explosions, including sailors who were severely burned. Only half of the men had escaped the ship with a life vest. As best they could in the dark, the surviving crew gathered in groups and floated together. The action of the waves and tide soon separated the scattered groups by miles.[268]

A few groups were lucky enough to find floating nets and rubber rafts dislodged from their ship to help keep them afloat,[269] but most men were left floating in the water, which proved to be a very dangerous place by the second day as another enemy discovered them: sharks! Hundreds of sharks began to attack the stranded sailors. The men kicked the sharks as they approached. Weakened men were separated from the group and became easy pickings for the deadly predators. While no exact number is known, it is possible that two hundred crewmen in the water were killed by shark attacks.[270]

Injury, exhaustion, hypothermia and dehydration were their other enemies. Men held on as long as they could, but as the days stretched on, hundreds more succumbed and slipped into watery graves.

The dwindling numbers of survivors clung to life with the hope of rescue—a rescue operation that, inexplicably, had not yet even begun. Unbeknownst to the imperiled crew, another tragedy had already taken place that would impact how many of them would survive. It was the tragedy of naval shore stations dismissing the S.O.S. transmissions that had been received from the ship.

The navy claimed, initially, that the S.O.S. messages had never been received by a ship or shore station. Years later, however, it was discovered in declassified records that, in fact, three different naval shore stations received the ship's emergency transmissions and failed to act on them. With the shore stations having dismissed the S.O.S. transmissions, the men's rescue came down to luck. And luck was slow in coming.[271]

Good fortune did finally come on August 2, when pilot Chuck Gwinn, flying one of two navy planes on reconnaissance missions, miraculously spotted some of the stranded men. Gwinn's crew dropped rafts and radioed coordinates for ships in the area to proceed to the men's location for rescue operations.[272]

Adrian Marks, pilot of a navy PBY Catalina amphibious plane with installed floats that allowed it to make sea landings, received the transmission of coordinates and flew to the area. He spotted groups of the men floating in the water with sharks nearby. Against orders from his superiors, Marks, a native of Frankfort, Indiana, landed his plane on the dangerous sea, which had twelve-foot swells, and came alongside a group of the men. Marks and his crew were credited with saving fifty-six of the stranded sailors who climbed in, hung on or were lashed to the wings of the plane while they awaited rescue from the ships that had been dispatched and were en route.[273]

Ship rescue operations began on August 3 and lasted for several days. There were seven navy ships that participated in the operation. When the rescue was completed, only 321 of the almost 900 crewmen who made it off the *Indianapolis* four days earlier were still alive.[274] The loss of almost 900 sailors made the sinking of the USS *Indianapolis* the worst U.S. naval disaster at sea in history. The rescued survivors were taken to Peleliu and later Guam for medical care before returning to the United States on the USS *Hollandia* in late September 1945.[275]

In 1960, fifteen years after the tragic sinking of their ship, 121 survivors of the USS *Indianapolis* attended their first reunion in the city of their ship's namesake.[276] During their time together, someone suggested a memorial to honor and remember their lost shipmates. The idea resonated and then simmered.[277] The subject of a memorial resurfaced at the next reunion in 1965.[278] This time, the discussion generated momentum. An exploratory committee was created to investigate the feasibility for such a project. The city of Indianapolis was the logical choice for a memorial. The survivors formed a not-for-profit corporation and later recruited a local Indianapolis architect, Joseph Fischer of Fischer Construction, to begin designing a memorial.[279]

The biggest hurdle initially was finding a suitable piece of property in Indianapolis for the memorial. The land search dragged on for years without success. Good news finally came in 1990 when the mayor of Indianapolis, William H. Hudnut III, announced his intent to donate to the survivors' organization prime property along the Indiana Central Canal that ran through downtown Indianapolis.[280] It was an ideal location, and it was the perfect time to capitalize on the growing publicity for the upcoming fiftieth anniversary of the war's end in 1995.

There were challenges right from the start in raising money for the memorial. The first challenge was its growing cost. The project's initial estimate was $500,000. By the time the memorial was completed in 1995, the cost had risen to $1 million.[281]

The second challenge was lack of public knowledge about the ship. It might seem strange that the citizens of Indianapolis could have forgotten or never heard of the ship named for the city. Almost five decades had passed, however, since the sinking of the *Indianapolis* forty-five years earlier. In the drive to get on with life after the war, most people had forgotten the role the USS *Indianapolis* played in ending the Pacific War. The *Enola Gay*, a B-29 Superfortress, received the attention for dropping the atomic bomb over Hiroshima. Few recalled, however, that the bomb had been delivered to Tinian by the *Indianapolis*.

Fortunately, Finneran and the survivors' organization had a local asset in their campaign to educate the public. Survivor Jimmy O'Donnell, a water tender third class, was the only native of the city of Indianapolis to survive the tragic sinking. He returned to Indianapolis after the war and became a firefighter in his hometown. He could tell the ship's story as a survivor and a local hero. O'Donnell accepted the role and traveled throughout the metropolitan area for five years, sharing the story of the *Indianapolis* and collecting funds for the memorial.[282] His effort, and that of many others, bore fruit. The $1 million was raised just in time to complete the memorial and tie the dedication into the fiftieth anniversary of the ship's sinking and the war's end.

The dedication for the USS *Indianapolis* Memorial took place on July 30, 1995, exactly fifty years after its sinking. The event drew approximately 3,500 people, including 107 survivors, who came to see the unveiling of Joseph Fischer's creation. What they saw when the drape was removed were black and gray granite pieces from California that Fischer used to fashion the twenty-one-ton structure in the general shape of a navy ship. Fischer pointed the bow of the ship structure westward toward the Pacific Ocean to honor the ship's crew who died in the middle of the Philippine Sea. He placed the monument on a base of Indiana limestone and adorned the black granite face of the memorial with a detailed white silhouette of the USS *Indianapolis*. On the back of the memorial, he listed the names of the crew of 1,197 men on board the ship at the time of its sinking, each name engraved with one-inch letters, the survivors identified by a star beside their names.[283]

Fischer wrapped the narrative of the USS *Indianapolis* story around the twenty-eight-foot-long base of the memorial.[284] He used the north side of the base to present general information on the ship: construction details, physical dimensions, engine type, armament description and its honorable résumé of service in the navy from 1932 to 1945. The text on the south side of the base, underneath the names of the ship's crew, summarized the tragic events that led to its sinking on July 30, 1945, and the long ordeal for those who made it off the ship and attempted to survive in the water.[285] He cut into the base of the memorial ten stars to represent the ten battle stars the *Indianapolis* received for its war service. Directly behind the granite ship, Fischer placed a high, curved wall with a water feature to represent the ship's bridge and to serve as an overlook for the memorial.[286]

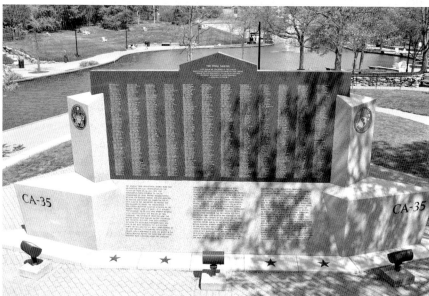

Top: Front of USS *Indianapolis* Memorial. *Ronald May.*

Bottom: Back of USS *Indianapolis* Memorial. *Ronald May.*

There was one feature of the memorial that was not visible to the crowd of onlookers. Buried beneath the memorial was a piece of the superstructure of the USS *Arizona*.[287] As the last navy ship to be sunk before the war's end, the USS *Indianapolis* became historically linked to the first ship that was sunk during the attack at Pearl Harbor, the battleship USS *Arizona*. The two ships became unintended timeline bookends for the American experience in the Second World War.

While the sunken ships are linked by the war's timeline, their respective memorials are linked by the common effort to honor their dead. Since the *Indianapolis* and most of its crew were lost in the middle of the Philippine Sea, the *Indianapolis* Memorial is, for most of the families of the deceased, the symbolic burial location for their loved ones. *Indianapolis* survivor Jimmy O'Donnell put it matter-of-factly: "It's the only tombstone they'll have."[288] The memorial with the engraved names of the dead is now a place where families and friends reach out to touch and do rubbings over the names of loved ones lost far out at sea. "Their grief requires closure," Finneran said, concerning the families. "Hopefully, this memorial will provide it." He added the prediction, "This is going to be their Vietnam Wall."[289]

The completion of the memorial seemingly changed the trajectory of publicity that had been lacking for the ship during the first fifty years after its sinking. The memorial leapfrogged from being a centerpiece for memory to being a launch pad for new ways of preserving the ship's story.

In 2007, the USS *Indianapolis* Gallery opened in the Indiana War Memorial. Through its exhibits, the gallery celebrates the proud history of the USS *Indianapolis*, tells the story of its fateful final voyage and rescue operation and helps preserve the memories of many of the ship's crew. One display case shows a dress white uniform of Thomas Leon Barksdale, a native of Seymour, Indiana. He was a fire controlman (third class) who had reported to the ship in the fall of 1943. Barksdale was among the nine hundred who made it off the *Indianapolis* before it sank, but he was one of the near six hundred who perished in the sea while awaiting rescue. His body, barely afloat with his waterlogged life vest, was discovered during rescue operations by the USS *Helm* on August 5. He was identified and then given sea burial.[290]

In 2009, the City of Indianapolis erected a bronze statue honoring James E. "Jimmy" O'Donnell, who died in 2013. The life-size statue of the young sailor was placed outside of City Market in downtown Indianapolis. It honors him for his service on the *Indianapolis* and preserves the story of the ship and its crew.

Yet another honor was bestowed on the ship in May 2011 when the Indiana state legislature passed a resolution to name Interstate 465, the loop circling the city, the USS *Indianapolis* Memorial Highway.

In 2017, billionaire Paul Allen's search crew discovered the *Indianapolis* resting three miles under the Philippine Sea, approximately 650 miles east of Leyte and west of Guam.[291] It remains there today, along with the remains of three hundred crewmen, almost eighty years after its sinking.

In December 2018, a resolution was passed in Congress for the entire crew of the *Indianapolis* to be honored collectively with a Congressional Gold Medal.[292]

The U.S. Navy contributed to the growing legacy of the heavy cruiser in October 2019 when, at the Port of Indiana–Burns Harbor, a new ship was commissioned and named USS *Indianapolis (LCS 17)*. A Littoral Combat Ship, and the fourth ship to bear the name of the city, it is homeported at the Naval Station in Mayport, Florida. Its motto, "Legacy of War," seems appropriate, given its predecessor's proud and tragic history.[293]

For the foreseeable future, the legacy of the USS *Indianapolis* will continue both on land, at the USS *Indianapolis* Memorial and at sea, in the naval service of LCS 17.[294]

16

CANDLES HOLOCAUST MUSEUM AND EDUCATION CENTER

The most horrific and tragic chapter of World War II was the murder of 6 million Jews, as well as millions of others, by the Nazis. One of the lesser-known atrocities committed during their reign of terror was the deadly medical and genetic experiments on 1,500 sets of Jewish twins at the Auschwitz Death Camp in Poland by the Nazi SS doctor Josef Mengele.

CANDLES Museum and Education Center in Terre Haute tells the personal story of two of those twins, Eva (Mozes) Kor and her sister, Miriam (Mozes) Zieger, who suffered through the terrible ordeal and survived. Born in 1934 in the village of Portz, Romania, the twins were the youngest of four daughters born to Alexander and Jaffa Mozes. They entered the world just as the Nazi Party had taken control of Germany and was spreading its campaign of hatred and discrimination toward European Jews. While the family enjoyed a time of relative peace for the first ten years of Eva's life, they lived under the growing threat of anti-Jewish fervor, especially after Romania joined the Axis Powers in 1940 and the village of Portz came under a Hungarian Nazi armed guard.[295]

Their lives changed forever in 1944 when the family was forcibly relocated by the Nazis from their home to a regional Jewish ghetto in Simleu Silvaniei, Romania. A few weeks later, the Mozes family, along with many other Jewish families, were loaded onto cattle cars and transported to the Auschwitz Death Camp in Poland.[296]

Stepping off the train and onto the infamous selection platform, the twins, tagged as subjects for Mengele's experiments, were immediately separated from the rest of the Mozes family. Eva and Miriam never again saw their parents or older sisters, who were put to death in the camp.[297]

Eva and Miriam became fresh recruits for Dr. Mengele's genetic experimentation on twins. For the next eight months, they were subjected to painful, degrading and often deadly genetic experimentation. Most of the twins in the camp died during the rigorous phases of experimentation.[298] Mengele was conducting the risky experiments to learn more about dominant genes in twins and how to manipulate them to bolster the reproduction of Germans, what he and most Germans considered to be the perfect Aryan race.[299]

At one point, Eva became very ill from an injection and, after two weeks in the Auschwitz infirmary, was almost sent to the gas chamber for extermination. Eva somehow willed herself to survive and get back to Miriam, who was living in one of the barracks for twins.[300]

Although twins received slightly better treatment than the rest of the Jews at Auschwitz, daily life was a struggle for survival, with inadequate food, crude living conditions and harsh weather. For eight long months, the Mozes twins struggled to stay alive.

The Auschwitz camp was finally liberated by the advancing Soviet army in late January 1945. At the time of liberation, only two hundred children were found to be alive of the three thousand twins who had been selected for the medical experimentation. Eva and Miriam were among the survivors.[301]

Following their release from the death camp, the twins, who had just turned eleven years old, looked for but didn't find anyone else in their family who had survived imprisonment at Auschwitz. For nine months, the Mozes twins were bounced around to three different refugee camps. They finally landed in Romania and were raised by an aunt.[302]

Both Eva and Miriam immigrated to Israel in 1950 at the age of sixteen. Eva later joined the Israeli army and met Michael Kor, an American tourist, who also happened to be a Holocaust survivor. They married in 1960 and came to the United States, settling in Terre Haute, Indiana, where they raised two children, Alex and Rina.[303] Eva became a U.S. citizen in 1965.[304]

In the early 1980s, Eva began searching for other Auschwitz twin survivors. She enlisted the help of her sister Miriam, who was still living in Israel. To further aid in their effort of reuniting Auschwitz twins, Eva founded Children of Auschwitz Nazi Deadly Lab Experiments Survivors (CANDLES) in 1984. The organization helped reconnect 122 Mengele twins scattered around the world and provided a support network for them.[305]

Eva returned to Auschwitz for the first time in 1984 to confront her past and tell the story of her family and the Mengele twins. For the rest of her life, she made periodic trips back to Auschwitz, often bringing friends and educators on the tour.[306] During one of her visits back in 1991, she and her sister Miriam stood in front of the barbed wire fence where a photograph of them had been taken upon their liberation in 1945.[307]

Miriam died from bladder cancer in 1993. The disease was caused by one of the mysterious injections she had received at Auschwitz. Miriam had almost died six years earlier of kidney disease, also caused by the medical experimentation during her childhood. Eva donated one of her kidneys to Miriam in 1987. The transplant allowed her to live for six more years.[308]

In 1995, fifty years after the liberation of Auschwitz and in memory of her sister Miriam, whose death she was still mourning, Eva Kor opened the CANDLES Holocaust Museum and Education Center in Terre Haute.[309] The mission of the museum is to "contribute to the empowerment of the world through hope, healing, respect, and responsibility by shining a light on the story of the Holocaust, Eva Kor, the Mengele twins, and other survivors."[310] Eva liked the acronym because of its reference to light; she wanted to illuminate the darkness of the Holocaust.

That same year, Eva did something else remarkable. She publicly pronounced forgiveness of the Nazis for the pain and suffering they caused

CANDLES Museum, exterior. *Ronald May.*

Auschwitz photo with platform exhibit. *Ronald May*.

her and her family at Auschwitz. Eva arranged to meet a former Nazi doctor named Dr. Hans Munch at the Auschwitz camp and personally deliver her declaration of forgiveness to him, as a former representative of the Nazi Party. Although he had not been at Auschwitz, Munch knew Dr. Mengele and was aware of the atrocities being done there. Acknowledging the guilt of the Nazi regime, he signed a public document testifying to the gas chamber being used to exterminate Jews at Auschwitz.[311]

Dr. Mengele, who escaped from Germany and later fled to South America under a false identity, somehow evaded capture for the rest of his life. He was never brought to justice for his criminal medical experiments on three thousand children. He died by accidental drowning in 1979 while swimming off the coast of Brazil. DNA tests of his remains in 1985 confirmed that he was the infamous Nazi doctor at Auschwitz.[312]

CANDLES Holocaust Museum and Education Center is Indiana's only Holocaust Museum and the only museum in the world dedicated to telling the story of Jewish twins subjected to medical experimentation during the Holocaust.[313]

While the museum has been popular, it also became a target for hatred and destruction. In 2003, an arsonist set fire to the museum. Undeterred by the tragic destruction and boosted by $300,000 of donations raised by the city, Eva Kor and the museum's leadership reopened their new and larger CANDLES museum in 2005.[314]

Today, through the photographs, documents, memorabilia, exhibits and audio-visual displays in the museum, visitors are introduced to the Mozes family and their tragic journey to Auschwitz. They also learn about the heinous work of Dr. Mengele and the thousands of twins who suffered and died from his cruel genetic experimentation. The museum also traces the adult lives of Eva and Miriam, who dedicated their lives to telling the story of this dark chapter of the Holocaust.

Perhaps most important of all, visitors are invited to consider and embrace the transformative power of forgiveness as they trace Eva's profound decision to pronounce it upon the very people who killed her family and almost killed her and Miriam. Her bold message is displayed at the end of the museum exhibits: "Anger and hate are seeds that germinate war. Forgiveness is a seed for peace. It is the ultimate act of self-healing."[315]

Eva Kor died on July 4, 2019, at the age of eighty-five. She was in Poland at the time of her death, leading a CANDLES tour to Auschwitz.[316] Her death, however, has not prevented her from personally sharing her story today.[317] Visitors can still get an interactive experience with her through the museum's new Dimensions in Testimony Interactive Theater, which opened in 2017. The theater shows realistic two-dimensional videos in the fashion of a hologram. In the presentation, Kor sits on a chair in her distinctive

Eva Kor, "Dimensions in Testimony" interactive exhibit. *Ronald May.*

blue pantsuit while photos from her life are projected beside her. She and a dozen other survivors traveled to a Los Angele studio in 2016, and each was placed inside a geodesic dome with lights and cameras that recorded them answering up to two thousand questions about their experiences during the Holocaust, as well as their lives before and after. Their "responses were indexed by keywords, which were then tied into newly developed voice [speech] recognition software."[318] The finished video product allows visitors to ask a broad range of questions and receive their answers from the survivors in real time, making it feel almost like a conversation.

CANDLES Holocaust Museum and Education Center is located at 1532 South Third Street, Terre Haute, Indiana.[319] It is well worth a visit. In addition to the exhibits and educational presentations, the museum also conducts annual tours to Auschwitz in memory of Eva.[320]

For more information, visit https://candlesholocaustmuseum.org.

17

VETERANS MEMORIAL MUSEUM

Brian Mundell loves military history. As he was growing up in Terre Haute, he cherished the stories told to him by his grandfather, a veteran of World War II. While in fourth grade, Mundell wrote a book report on the Japanese attack at Pearl Harbor. He still has it today. At the age of twenty-six, he tried to enlist in the Marine Corps Reserve. A problem with his blood sugar prevented him from joining. But his interest in military history continued, and he began collecting military memorabilia.[321]

In 2004, Mundell traveled to Normandy, France, for the sixtieth anniversary of the D-Day invasion. That experience increased his drive to acquire more military items, most of which he purchased. It wasn't until 2011, when the lease of the building he owned adjacent to his business went unfilled, that he thought seriously of using the space as a museum for his growing collection.[322]

On Veterans Day in 2012, Mundell opened the Veterans Memorial Museum of Terre Haute. Located just east of downtown Terre Haute at 1129 Wabash Avenue, the building is next to his cabinet business, Superior Kitchen and Bath.

Right from the start, Mundell wanted to do more than just display objects of war history in his museum; he wanted to also tell the stories of the people associated with those objects. That is why so many of his museum items include the names and hometowns of those who owned, used or acquired the pieces of combat history, as well as photos of them.[323]

Veterans Memorial Museum. *Ronald May*.

That is also why Mundell does as much biographical research as possible on the people behind the pieces.[324] He has such a love for veterans and their stories that he has also interviewed them for the Library of Congress, Veterans History Project.[325]

The museum features combat service artifacts from World War I through the more recent wars in Iraq and Afghanistan. The museum pieces—half of them were purchased by Mundell and half have been donated by veterans and their families—are mostly honoring Wabash River Valley veterans from communities like Clinton, Mt. Carmel, Princeton, Terre Haute and Vincennes. "I appreciate the fact they entrust me to display their family's items and try to preserve that and honor their veterans," Mundell said in a 2017 interview marking the five-year anniversary of his museum.[326]

Mundell's museum is filled with the stuff of everyday life in combat. This includes helmets, uniforms, photos, flags, maps, weapons, medals, letters and a host of items that other museums don't include. At least one third of the museum features items from World War II. In addition to memorabilia from Allied forces, he also displays German and Japanese artifacts, including flags, helmets, weapons, propaganda and personal gear from individual soldiers.

The best of his World War II collection is, in this author's opinion, the ordinary personal items of service members. The display of Richard Martin is one example. Martin, a Rockville, Indiana native, was serving with the army at Pearl Harbor when the Japanese attacked. He took some

World War II Nazi flag, with Allied soldier signatures. *Ronald May.*

personal photos in the aftermath of the destruction and managed to secure a few pieces of metal from a Japanese plane that crashed into the army barracks. Both Martin's photos and the Japanese plane pieces are on exhibit at the museum and provide the visitor with a fresh glimpse into the Day of Infamy.[327]

The Gerstmeyer Honor Roll is another unique piece of local World War II history. This large glass-enclosed wooden display case contains all 1,600 names of Gerstmeyer Technical High School students who served in World War II. A gold star appears next to the names of servicemen who were killed in action. The display, designed by drafting teacher James Royer and his students and built with the help of other teachers and students, once hung prominently in the Terre Haute school, paying tribute to those who served and those who died. Glancing at it today, the visitor gains a deeper appreciation for the great number of young men from Terre Haute who went off to war, some of whom never returned.[328]

Gerstmeyer honor roll, World War II. *Ronald May.*

Japanese artwork is featured in another display. Navy Seabee veteran Ivan Williamson, a native of nearby Le Roy, Illinois, served on the island of Guam as a storekeeper at the war's conclusion. Some Japanese POWs were assigned to Williamson to assist him with maintaining twenty-nine warehouses of supplies for the 6th Fleet. One of those prisoners was a gifted artist. Through hand signals, he asked Williamson for cloth and pencils that he could use for drawing. The man created beautiful colored pencil sketch drawings on pillowcases and any other cloth he could find for his "canvas." Three of his pillowcase sketches are included in the Williamson display. Two of them feature Japanese women in traditional dress, and the third is a rendering of Betty Grable in a bathing suit. Landscape features and Japanese temples are included in the drawings, along with Japanese writing. The humane side of the former enemy is revealed in these colorful sketches. Williamson obviously thought enough of them that he brought them home from the war.[329]

As fascinating as the Japanese pencil sketches are, the display of an American pilot's literary work is even more interesting. You must look carefully to see it because his handwritten poetry is on the back of carefully unfolded cigarette wrappers. The poet was Second Lieutenant Roger B. Withers of Terre Haute. Withers was a B-17 pilot serving in the European

Lieutenant Roger Withers display, with poems. *Ronald May.*

Theater with the 8th Air Force, 388th Bomb Group, 562nd Bomb Squadron. His plane was shot down on May 28, 1944, on his twelfth mission while bombing Germany.[330] He was taken prisoner and spent the remainder of the war in German Stalag VII-A Prisoner of War Camp in Moosburg, Germany.[331] While waiting for the war to end, he wrote on the back side of American cigarette wrappers that were shipped in Red Cross packages and penned at least twenty-eight lighthearted poems. His subjects ranged from planes to people and often included a reference to his imprisonment. "Why a Kriegie?" is a sample of his self-effacing and humorous style as he reflects on how he went from pilot to prisoner:[332]

> *I wandered as a lonely cloud*
> *That floats on hills in straggling bits*
> *When all at once I saw a crowd*
> *A host of yellow Messerschmitts*
> *And now interned for the duration*
> *I wish I had not lost formation.*

In addition to his poems, the Withers display also includes personal photographs, his POW ID papers and dog tag, his pilot's logbook, journal, maps, medals and other mementoes. Withers spent one year as a POW. He was liberated from the German prison camp in the late spring of 1945 and returned home to Indiana.[333]

If Mundell's many displays are the inner contents of the museum's stories, the museum's exterior is the book's cover, designed to capture attention and invite people inside to learn more. It does both. Wanting to make sure that people spotted the museum on a concentrated stretch of businesses along Wabash Avenue, Mundell had a large mural painted on the museum's exterior wall facing the street. It is illuminated at night. Created by artist Jim Shepard, the mural includes iconic images from the U.S. involvement in twentieth-century wars from World War I to the present.[334]

In 2022, to celebrate the museum's tenth anniversary, Mundell added another outdoor mural. This one is a memorial wall to honor the 1,133 men and women from the seven counties around Terre Haute who were killed in combat from World War I to the present. The names appear by county in white letters on clear Plexiglas panels. The panels were installed over a mural by artist Becky Hochhalter. It features the background of a U.S. flag and the foreground of a combat soldier's silhouette as he is kneeling in honor toward a fallen soldier memorial: a helmet resting on the stock of an overturned M-16. Near the top of the mural are the bold words "They Died That We Might Live" and a quote from Jesus in the Gospel of John: "Greater love has no man than this, that a man lay down his life for his friends."[335]

It is the essence of a service member's sacrifice that Mundell seems most interested in conveying to visitors and future generations. "What I pride myself on trying to do here, is to honor the average everyday soldier," he explained. "If it opens anyone's eyes to the sacrifice that the veterans had to go through, then I guess I've done my job here."[336]

Mundell has done his job and then some. Unable to serve in uniform, he has helped preserve the stories of those who have served. And in putting his money, time and efforts behind honoring them, he has demonstrated his own honor. My advice to the reader is to go check out the museum and be sure to meet Mundell.

For more information, visit https://veteransmuseumofterrehaute.com.

18

CAMP ATTERBURY

While there were many military bases in Indiana during the 1940s, none grew so large or became as significant as Camp Atterbury in Central Indiana. During World War II, the expansive base trained four army divisions for combat, provided state-of-the-art medical care for thousands of wounded battlefront soldiers and housed both Italian and German enemy prisoners of war. With two army airfields within thirty miles of its location, Camp Atterbury and the U.S. Army Air Forces made South Central Indiana the busiest and largest military presence in the state.

CAMP ATTERBURY TRAINING BASE

In January 1941, the U.S. War Department considered possible sites in Indiana for an army training base to handle the influx of trainees who were flooding the army following the passage of President Roosevelt's Selective Service Act in October 1940. The land near Edinburgh, Indiana, seemed ideal. Located thirty miles south of Indianapolis and twelve miles north of Columbus, the area was both flat and hilly—the variation made for good training ground—and it was near big cities, excellent roads and well-linked railways. The federal government purchased large tracts of the property through mandatory sales and forced relocations.[337]

Like most military installations in the Midwest, the land for the new base was formerly farm fields. More than forty thousand acres of good farmland were spread across the southern part of Johnson County and the northern parts of Bartholomew and Brown Counties. Drama and heartache ensued as farms, farmhouses, schools, churches, cemeteries and even a small town of thirteen residents were swallowed up by the government land acquisitions throughout 1941. It cost the government almost $4 million and resulted in the dislocation of five hundred farm families.[338]

The base was named Camp Atterbury to honor Indiana native General William Wallace Atterbury for his distinguished service as director of transportation of the American Expeditionary Forces during the First World War. Construction began in February 1942 and continued for six months.[339] Army plans called for building facilities to train a full army division, some forty thousand soldiers.[340]

When completed, the expansive camp included "1,780 buildings and provided housing to 44,159 officers and soldiers, including: 499 enlisted men's barracks, 40 Bachelor Officer Quarters (BOQs), 23 Womens' Army Corp (WAC) barracks, 61 Prisoners-of-War (POW) barracks, 193 mess halls, 12 chapels, five service clubs, three officers' clubs, six theatres, four gymnasiums, four swimming pools, and one hospital and convalescent center."[341]

Combat training necessitated having enough firing ranges—there were twenty-one in the camp—which accommodated the firing of all the different

Camp Atterbury rock carved by Italian POW Libero Puccini. *Ronald May.*

weapons used by an army division, from a .45-caliber pistol up to an artillery weapon that had a range of nine miles. Once soldiers mastered use of their assigned weapons in small unit exercises, they trained as a division on one of five combat ranges where realistic battlefront conditions were simulated. The base also had a mock town called Tojoburg, which consisted of thirty buildings and dummies. Smaller division units used Tojoburg for practice on approaching a town in enemy territory.[342]

Even before construction was completed, the newly reactivated 83rd Infantry Division reported to Camp Atterbury in August 1942 and became the first army division to train at the military installation. By this point, the base consisted of 1,700 buildings and had cost $86 million. Following its training, the 83rd ("Thunderbolt") Division departed for Europe in April 1944 and saw combat service in France, Luxembourg and Germany.[343]

Three more divisions trained at Camp Atterbury from 1942 to 1944. The 92nd ("Buffalo Soldiers") Division arrived in October 1942 and eventually was sent to serve in the Italian campaign. The 30th ("Old Hickory") Division reported in November 1943 and was quickly sent to England two months later to begin the buildup for the Normandy invasion. Finally, the 106th ("Golden Lions") Division arrived at Atterbury in February 1944 and, ten months later, found itself fighting for its life during the surprise attack of German forces in Belgium in the Battle of the Bulge. The division lost almost 9,000 casualties in the first month of that battle. Throughout the war, close to 275,000 men in more than one hundred military units trained for combat at Camp Atterbury, while thousands of other soldiers came for advanced training.[344]

WAKEMAN GENERAL HOSPITAL

While Camp Atterbury was training soldiers for combat, the station hospital on base was growing to accommodate a much larger mission. It was initially built as a 1,700-bed hospital to handle the medical needs of the army personnel training at the camp, as well as to provide experience for those training in medical ratings. In March 1944, the War Department announced that Atterbury Hospital was to become a general hospital for treating the wounded from overseas combat. This meant expanding the footprint of the hospital and creating fields of specialists to include burn treatment, neurology, orthopedics and plastic surgery.[345]

Wakeman Hospital, under construction. *Atterbury-Bakalar Museum.*

Among the expanded medical staff that came to Camp Atterbury were women. The Women's Army Corps (WACs) made a significant contribution in the treatment of wounded soldiers arriving from the front. The first group of WACs arrived at Camp Atterbury in March 1943 and filled various clerical roles. With the increasing size and mission of the base hospital, medical sections of WAC units began arriving to support the care of wounded at the hospital. This included a detachment of 141 African American women who were assigned to the hospital. The WACs' Medical Department Enlisted Technician's School was moved from Arkansas to Camp Atterbury in July 1944, resulting in more than 3,800 women receiving their medical training at Atterbury Hospital.[346]

The new focus of the expanded hospital also resulted in a new name, Wakeman General Hospital, named for Colonel Frank B. Wakeman, who received some of his education in Indiana and served during World War I as an infantry officer. Following the war, he earned his medical degree in Indiana and then returned to the army as a doctor, later rising to the rank of colonel.[347]

By August 1944, a steady stream of casualties had begun arriving at Wakeman Hospital from the European Theater. Flown across the ocean in C-47 cargo planes to the Regional Station Hospital at Mitchell Field, New York, the final leg of their journey was a twelve-mile ride in an ambulance from Atterbury Army Airfield in nearby Columbus.[348]

Plastic surgery section and Colonel Blocker Jr., Wakeman General Hospital. *Camp Atterbury Museum.*

One of the army surgeons meeting the wounded at Wakeman General Hospital was Truman G. Blocker Jr. The Mississippi native had spent most of his life in Texas, where he also earned his MD degree from the University of Texas Medical Branch at Galveston. After several years of surgical practice, he became certified with the American Board of Plastic Surgery in 1942. That same year, he enlisted in the Army Air Corps as a medical surgeon and later transferred to the army.[349]

Blocker reported to Wakeman General Hospital in the summer of 1944 (just before the wounded began arriving from Normandy) and became chief of plastic surgery and later chief of surgery. His revolutionary medical skill combined with his effective administrative gifts proved equal to the challenges of a hospital that grew from two thousand patients to six thousand patients and from treating colds, illness and basic injuries to treating severe burns and orthopedic injuries from the battlefield. What many wounded needed—extensive plastic surgery—was exactly what Blocker and his recruited team of specialist surgeons excelled in. He made a national name for himself and the hospital. He and his medical team were so successful in treating the burned and injured with plastic surgery that upon his discharge, he was awarded the Legion of Merit, an award rarely given, and almost never to a medical officer.[350]

The capacity for patients at Wakeman General Hospital reached ten thousand in early 1945 and remained at that level until the end of the war with Japan in September 1945. In the short span of seventeen months (April 1944 through August 1945), more than eighty-five thousand wounded patients received their medical care at Wakeman. Not only were lives saved, but thousands of soldiers disfigured by war also received specialized plastic surgery, allowing them to return to their homes more whole than when they first left the battlefield.[351] Following the war's conclusion, Wakeman General Hospital continued treating patients until it was closed at the end of 1946 by the War Department.[352]

PRISONER OF WAR CAMP [353]

Less than a year after opening, Camp Atterbury constructed an Internment Camp for Prisoners of War. Built on forty-five acres west of the main training area, the camp held three thousand prisoners in a secure compound of one hundred buildings surrounded by a stockade and barbed wire.[354]

The first prisoners arriving at Camp Atterbury in April 1943 were Italian soldiers who had fought in North Africa and surrendered to the Allies near Tunis. By September, the prison population had reached its capacity at three thousand men, mostly Italians.[355] One of the POWs, a stone craftsman named Libero Puccini, was tasked with carving the name of Camp Atterbury and the date 1942 into a large stone (see page 122). It remains in place today (commonly known as the "Atterbury Rock") at the top of a hill at the entrance of the camp property along the north side of Old Hospital Road. Puccini returned to America after the war and became a U.S. citizen.[356]

The prisoners' new home at the internment camp included relatively comfortable sleeping, dining and recreational areas. What it didn't have was a chapel. The Italian prisoners sought to build one with the encouragement from their Roman Catholic chaplain, Father Maurice Imhoff. They received permission from the camp's commanding officer, Lieutenant Colonel John Gammel, to create a chapel from the materials that were left over from the camp's construction: cement blocks, bricks, wood, mortar and stucco.[357]

Using their free time—the men had jobs during the day either on the camp's grounds or out in the community on farms or factories[358]—the prisoners, many of whom were skilled workers and artisans, erected an eleven-by-sixteen-foot chapel. They built the shell of the chapel from brick and stucco and painted it a Mediterranean blue. They made a gable roof and adorned it with a cross. The floor was constructed to look like the terracotta tile from their homeland by putting lines in the concrete in the shape of squares and painting it red. Artisans painted detailed frescoes on the walls and ceiling. They painted the eye of God on the ceiling and a cross with a cherub over each side of the altar. Other frescoes on the side walls included a Dove of Peace, Madonna, St. Anthony of Padua and Francis of Assisi. They dressed the altar, made from a wooden crate, with a painted faux-marble texture. The paint was created by using dyes from plants, berries and even the prisoners' own blood.[359]

The chapel was completed and dedicated to the Blessed Mother in the summer of 1943.[360] It was christened the "Chapel in the Meadow." Although humble in size, the three-sided structure provided a roof over Chaplain Imhoff as he led Mass. It became a sacred place for worship and a symbol of hope for the prisoners living so far from home. Here they could come on their free time for private worship, pray for their loved ones back home in Italy and thank God that they had survived the war. The sacred space was also a touch of home for the prisoners. With its Italian-style blue stucco walls and its Italian-inspired artwork in the frescoes, the chapel connected the prisoners to the religion and culture of their native homeland.

With Italy's capitulation in late 1943, the Italian POWs began to be released and repatriated to Italy in 1944. The last of the Italian prisoners left Camp Atterbury on May 4, 1944. Days later, German prisoners of war began arriving at Camp Atterbury. Their population swelled to almost nine thousand by October. They remained at the internment camp until after Germany's surrender in May 1945.[361]

In June 1946, the prison compound was torn down. The only building left intact was the Chapel in the Meadow, spared through the efforts of the wife of the commander in charge of the demolition and resale of the camp.[362] As years went by, the chapel was neglected and eventually fell into a state of disrepair. It was finally restored in 1988 by the Indiana National Guard at a cost of $30,000.[363] It remains today at its original but now isolated location on a serene, grassy area shaded by large trees around its perimeter. Visitors can walk up to the open side of the chapel, which is now covered with Plexiglas, and look in at the chancel once created by the hands and hearts of

Restored Chapel in the Meadow, Camp Atterbury. *Ronald May.*

Italian POWs. Some of the former POWs and their families have returned to the Chapel of the Meadow during reunion visits to Central Indiana.

The Chapel in the Meadow is located on Stone Arch Road, two miles west and one mile north of the Camp Atterbury Welcome Center. Small road signs are posted to help with directions. It's worth the seek-and-find adventure to visit it.

Camp Atterbury Today

Following World War II, Camp Atterbury served as a major military discharge center before it was inactivated. It was reactivated during the Korean and Vietnam Conflicts. In September 1976, the base became an Army National Guard Training Site and continued in that capacity until the 1990s. Today, Camp Atterbury is used by active and reserve forces of all branches from around the country to train and prepare for mobilization.[364]

The Camp Atterbury Museum, part of the Welcome Center, is just east of the main gate on Old Hospital Road. The items on display—including photos, papers, uniforms and artifacts—preserve the history of the base as well as the former hospital and POW camp.

There is also an outdoor area west of the Welcome Center that displays military vehicles from World War II. In the center of the outdoor viewing area is a Veterans Memorial Wall with the seals, titles and information on the divisions that once trained there. In front of the wall is a lone statue of a World War II soldier on a pedestal. His right arm is down at his side, holding his carbine; his left arm is outstretched with his hand pointing forward, perhaps toward the combat theaters that the men had trained for and were soon to enter. In front of the soldier is a reflecting pool and fountain that draw attention to the memorial and invite visitors to pause and consider the many thousands who, after training at Camp Atterbury, courageously headed off to war. A walkway of memorial bricks wraps around the water feature.

Visitors to Camp Atterbury will find much to explore and learn about its World War II contribution and its ongoing significance today.

For more information, visit https://www.atterburymuscatatuck.in.ng.mil/About/Museums.

19

JAPANESE BAN MEMORIAL

pologies come in different ways. Some are verbal, some are conveyed on paper and others are more official institutional statements preserved on historical displays and meant to serve as a public and permanent record. Indiana University in Bloomington, Indiana, chose all three ways to finally express its regret for banning the enrollment of twelve Japanese American students between 1942 and 1945. The background to that story is one of the saddest chapters in American history.

In February 1942, following the Japanese attack at Pearl Harbor, President Roosevelt signed Executive Order 9066, which authorized commanders of the West Coast military zones to remove any persons they deemed a threat. Lieutenant General John L. Dewitt, leader of the Western Defense Command, used that authority to forcibly move the Japanese living on the West Coast, permitting them to take only what they could carry, and incarcerate them in relocation camps. Within months after the order was issued, approximately 122,000 Japanese residents, 70,000 of whom were American citizens, were removed from their homes and interned for the next several years.[365]

The Kanno family of Seattle, Washington, was among those unfortunate thousands of Japanese displaced and interned. Kyuma Kanno and his wife, Kikuyo, were both immigrants from Japan. They loved America but were unable to become citizens because the Immigration Act of 1924 prevented it. The couple had three American-born children: Mary and twins Jean and John.

Kanno family. Jean is at the bottom right. *Jean Kanno Umemura.*

Following the December 7, 1941 Japanese attack on Pearl Harbor, the loyalty of Japanese Americans progressively became suspect by the U.S. government and the communities in which they lived. Contrary to the rising paranoia, there was no lack of loyalty to America in the Kanno family or most of the other Japanese living on the West Coast. "We were so Americanized by then that we felt Japan was an enemy," Jean stated during an interview with the author. "As much as we loved our relatives [back in Japan], the three of us [siblings] were Americans. We were staunch about that. Our parents never scolded us for that. We would say the pledge [Pledge of Allegiance] at school until the very last day we were allowed to attend school. I used to look in the mirror and say, 'Am I really Japanese?' I couldn't believe it, because in my heart I felt so American, and I felt I surely looked like an American."[366]

In the weeks after the Pearl Harbor attack, life for the Kanno family and other West Coast Japanese became increasingly restricted. First there were curfews and driving limits. Then rumors began circulating of a possible evacuation.[367] The rumors were confirmed by President Roosevelt's Executive Order 9066 on February 19, 1942. Officials posted signs in public places throughout Seattle directing Japanese residents (including college students at West Coast universities) to report on a certain date between April and May to specified transportation sites in the city for their mandatory evacuation.

The Kannos' daughter Jean, a ninth-grade student at the time, recalled her family's heartbreak at their forced departure. "They made us get rid of everything," she said. "Our home and all our belongings. My father had to give up his business. It was hard. My parents had worked so hard to get where they were. I had to give up my book collection and all the things that were dear to me. I even had a doll collection, and I couldn't take that with me. We had to leave our friends. It was so sad. We couldn't take any personal belongings with us. We had kittens. I had to give up my piano lessons. We cried."[368]

The Kannos and other Japanese families living in Seattle and western Washington were taken initially to the Puyallup Assembly Center, thirty-five miles south of Seattle. They remained there for several months before being transported on a thirty-hour train ride to their permanent new "home" at Camp Minidoka in southern Idaho.

The Minidoka Relocation Center was one of ten internment camps in the western states of California, Arizona, Idaho, Utah, Wyoming and Colorado. Two camps were in Arkansas. The camps, which were hastily built wooden barracks, were in isolated and inhospitable places.

Camp Minidoka was a city of six hundred bare wooden structures covered with tar paper and spread over 946 acres of high desert. It was designed to accommodate ten thousand people, but that number was possible only by forcing inhabitants to live in tight, overcrowded spaces. Each barracks held multiple families and provided only fifty square feet of living space per family member. The rooms were barren, save an army cot for each person and a coal-burning stove for heat. Each block of barracks had mess, laundry and recreation halls.[369] There was also a public sanitary building, which offered no partitions for privacy. "It was horrible," Jean recalled. "You never got used to it."[370]

After some months, the camp's schools opened in designated barracks. Jean and her brother attended the camp's Hunt Jr./Sr. High School, graduating from there in the spring of 1944.[371]

By late 1942, the U.S. War Department and the War Relocation Agency had recognized their error in judgment in forcing the evacuation of the Japanese and interning them in camps. But there was no quick or easy way to release them since military authorities and community leaders didn't want them back on the West Coast. Camp directors didn't release a family unless they had a sponsor who could guarantee them a job and a place to live.[372] The easiest way out of the camps for high school graduates was finding a college or university to accept them as students. But this proved equally difficult, as so few universities opened their doors to Japanese enrollees.[373]

The Kanno family's eventual release from Camp Minidoka came indirectly through the University of Michigan accepting their elder daughter's enrollment into the School of Music. Mary had avoided internment at Minidoka in 1942 when the camp opened because she was already a student at Washington State University in Pullman, Washington—it was far enough east to be outside of the exclusion zone. While attending a conference in Wisconsin in the summer of 1944, she met a Baptist minister from Ann Arbor, Michigan, named Chester Loucks. Learning that Mary's family was interned at Camp Minidoka, he pledged his help in finding them a home and jobs in Ann Arbor. He advised Mary to enroll at the University of Michigan. She was accepted, and some months later, the Kanno family were released and reunited with Mary in Ann Arbor.[374]

While the University of Michigan offered enrollment to select Japanese students like Mary during the war, Indiana University (IU) in Bloomington did not.[375] In May 1942, the university's board of trustees issued a ban on accepting any students of Japanese descent.[376] The ban, which lasted until September 1945, barred the enrollment of at least twelve Japanese American students who had applied to IU during the war years.[377]

In 2018, fourth-generation Japanese American student Eric Langowski was in his last semester at Indiana University when he discovered IU's ban on Japanese student enrollment during the war. Remembering that his grandmother had gained her freedom from internment through her acceptance of enrollment at a university in Kansas, he organized a Day of

Remembrance event on the IU campus to coincide with the February 19 date of President Roosevelt's Executive Order of 1942. During that event, he formally requested that IU issue an apology for its ban on Japanese students.[378] He later wrote an extensive report on the ban, which was published in the June 2019 *Indiana Magazine of History*.

Two years later, on February 19, 2020, Langowski again issued a plea for the Indiana University Board of Trustees to offer a formal apology for the ban. This time, he handed the board a signed petition that had the backing of the Japanese American Citizens League (JACL) National Council.[379]

In November 2021, IU officially addressed the university's discrimination against the twelve Japanese American students who were denied admission. IU officials declared that the university would host a Day of Remembrance Panel Discussion in February 2022, as well as offer a new course focused on Japanese internment during the war. They also established the Masuji Miyakawa scholarship for twelve underrepresented students (representing the twelve Japanese students who had been banned from admission during the war) and created a commemorative space that publicly acknowledges IU's regret for the ban.[380]

The commemorative space includes a white boulder with an attached plaque and a bench in a small triangular green space between the Herman B.

Japanese Ban Commemorative Space, Indiana University. *Ronald May.*

Wells Library and the Hamilton Lugar School of Global and International Studies on the campus of Indiana University. The space is located on the south side of Tenth Street, next to North Eagleson Avenue.

The Historic Landmark plaque on the boulder reads:

> *This commemorative space is dedicated to the Japanese American students who were wrongly denied admission to Indiana University between 1942 and 1945. Indiana University regrets its failure to meet the needs of these students, for whom college would have meant freedom from prisons in which they, together with 120,000 other Japanese Americans, were forcibly incarcerated. The racial hatred that drove their unjust imprisonment is antithetical to the fundamental values of Indiana University, and this space is intended as a reminder of our shared commitment to social justice and equity. Dedicated November 12, 2021.*

While the plaque is small, its presence and intent convey the power behind three small words that Langowski and thousands of other Japanese have been waiting to hear and see: "We are sorry."[381]

POSTSCRIPT FOR INDIANA UNIVERSITY AND THE UMEMURAS

In the fall semester of 1946, Indiana University accepted the enrollment of its first Japanese American student since the war ban. Others soon followed.[382] One year later, Japanese American graduate student George Makoto Umemura enrolled in the MBA program at IU. Hailing from Seattle, like Jean, George had also spent time at Camp Minidoka before gaining acceptance at Ohio Wesleyan University in Delaware, Ohio. On August 12, 1950, Jean Kanno married George Umemura and moved to Bloomington. After completing his MBA at Indiana University in 1948, George enrolled in the doctoral program at the IU School of Business and, while working on his degree, taught courses to MBA students. He graduated with his doctorate in business in 1952. The Umemuras eventually settled in Indianapolis and raised three children. In their retirement, they traveled to area schools and shared their Japanese internment experiences.[383]

20

ATTERBURY ARMY AIR FIELD AND ATTERBURY-BAKALAR MUSEUM

The Atterbury Army Air Field (AAAF) outside Columbus, Indiana, was built on two thousand acres of farmland in mid-1942. The goal for the airfield was integrated air-ground combat training with army division forces at nearby Camp Atterbury. The combined training never materialized. Instead, the airfield endured four name changes and many different starts, stalls, stops and changes to its intended mission in the first few years.[384]

It wasn't until March 1944 that Atterbury Army Air Field settled into a sustained mission of training glider pilots for the Troop Carrier Command.[385] Columbus-area farmers sometimes got a close-up look at the gliders and pilots as they occasionally made unintended landings in the farmers' fields. The peak of glider pilot training at AAAF came in March 1945 when 745 takeoffs and landings were recorded in one day.[386]

The glider used by the U.S. Army Air Forces was the WACO CG-4A.[387] These gliders—there were 13,900 built and delivered—were manufactured at a cost of $15,000 each. They were made of wood, fabric and some steel. They measured 48 feet in length, stood 12.7 feet in height and had a wingspan of just over 48 feet. When fully loaded, they weighed 7,500 pounds. The gliders had room in their cargo holds for several different types of loads, including "13 soldiers, a jeep and four soldiers, a 105mm howitzer and three soldiers, an ammunition trailer, six wounded on stretchers and one medic, a small bulldozer, or even three mules."[388]

Inside a glider cockpit, Atterbury-Bakalar Museum. *Ronald May*.

The gliders were flown by two pilots and towed by C-47 cargo planes via a 350-foot rope. When the gliders neared their destination, the tow rope was released, and the gliders began their fast descent to the ground. Pilots of the gliders could steer and turn, but they could not stop their steady descent. They did their best to control the landing of their aircraft, but doing so without engines, and in fields fraught with natural and enemy-placed obstacles, often meant that the gliders broke apart on landing. Sadly, this resulted in the loss of life for some of the glider crew, as well as damage to equipment. Despite the risk of catastrophic crashes, many gliders made relatively safe landings and successfully delivered their forces or equipment to their objectives.[389]

Beginning with the invasion of Sicily in July 1943, glider units played key roles in delivering troops and equipment behind enemy lines in Europe. Throughout the war, the U.S. military used 4,003 gliders in eight different air assault missions. While almost 517 gliders were used for the Normandy invasion, an even greater number of gliders were used for Operation Market Garden in Holland (1,900) and Operation Varsity in the Rhine River regions of Germany (906). A total of 216 glider pilots died during these operations.[390]

Bloomington, Indiana native William "Bruce" Dalton was one of those glider pilots serving in Europe. He was born in 1914 and graduated from

Bloomington High School.[391] In 1942, at the age of twenty-seven, he enlisted in the Army Reserve and began the flight glider pilot program in Bloomington. "I was 27 years old and eligible for the draft, and I thought being a glider pilot would be better than walking," recalled Dalton during a 2004 interview for the Library of Congress's Veterans History Project.[392]

Bruce Dalton. *Atterbury-Bakalar Museum.*

On September 8, 1942, he was called up for active duty. For the next twenty months, he completed basic, primary and advanced glider training at several different army airfields. He also waited around a lot while other glider pilot classes ahead of him finished their training. After completing ninety hours of flight training, he became a commissioned flight officer/pilot with the rank of second lieutenant.

Assigned to the 43rd Troop Carrier Squadron, 315th Troop Carrier Group, he arrived in England in the summer of 1944 to prepare for combat flight operations. He got his chance to fly a combat mission into Holland in September 1944 for Operation Market Garden, the largest airborne assault of World War II. "I took a jeep trailer and eight medics," recalled Dalton in his interview. His squadron landed in a field with other gliders under gunfire.[393] The massive operation was designed for Allied paratroopers to secure key bridges in Holland and quickly penetrate Germany from the north. The operation ultimately failed, and the war dragged on for another eight months.

Dalton survived the war and returned to his wife and son in mid-1945. They made their home in Columbus, Indiana, where Dalton eventually owned and operated two men's clothing stores.[394]

The training of glider pilots was not the last or arguably even the most important mission at AAAF. In August 1944, the airfield began receiving C-47 air transports of injured service members who were flown in from the European Theater after a stop at Mitchell Field in New York. From there, it was a four-and-a-half-hour flight to Indiana. The proximity of the army's Wakeman General Hospital at Camp Atterbury, only twelve miles away, made the Atterbury Army Airfield an obvious choice as a landing and transfer site for the wounded. Most of the casualties came from England, but some were also flown from France. After touching down at Atterbury Air Base, the patients were transported by ambulance to Wakeman, arriving within one hour of landing. Receiving and transporting the wounded continued throughout the final twelve months of the war.[395]

At the end of the war, AAAF became inactive but remained on standby status. Reactivated in 1949, it was used during the Korean War and continued to operate in a reserve status through the Vietnam War. In 1954, the name of the base was changed to Bakalar Air Force Base (BAFB) to honor World War II pilot John Edmond Bakalar, a Hammond, Indiana native who was killed in action over France on September 1, 1944. In 1970, all military operations at BAFB were shut down, and in 1971 the Columbus Regional Airport took over the airfield.[396] But the memory of Atterbury Army Air Field was not forgotten.

In 1992, the Atterbury-Bakalar Museum was built on part of the former airfield to preserve its memory. The museum dedicated an expansion in 2014.[397]

Bruce Dalton, the former glider pilot from Bloomington, never trained at AAAF, but he became one of the most active volunteers at the museum for two decades. He pursued a relentless goal of finding and securing an authentic glider nose/cockpit to display at the museum.[398] He then helped raise funds for a future museum expansion that included a media center. The media center was dedicated on April 25, 2010. It was named the William "Bruce" Dalton Media Center.[399]

Inside the museum, you will find the nose of the WACO CG-4A glider that Dalton secured as a signature display for the museum. An exhibit tells the story of glider training and missions. Other exhibits tell the history of the airfield and showcase some of the units and people who trained at the former army airfield and later Atterbury-Bakalar Air Force Base. There is a cutaway of a typical barracks in the 1940s, an art exhibit of aircraft, a scale aircraft models display and a rotating beacon from the original airfield. Visitors will also find an Indiana Aviation Hall of Fame wall that displays the photographs and service summaries of Hoosier pilots who served in the army and air force, including four women. The museum also has an impressive library.

Less than two blocks from the museum is a former barracks building from Atterbury Army Air Base that was converted to a chapel during the Korean War. It is the only building that remains from the former World War II airfield. Restored from 1995 to 1998, the chapel was renamed the Jeanne Norbeck Memorial Chapel in May 1998.[400]

While Norbeck didn't have any direct connection to Atterbury Army Air Field, she did have a lot to do with the city of Columbus and military flying.

Above: Jeanne Lewellen Norbeck Memorial Chapel. *Ronald May*.

Left: Jeanne Lewellen Norbeck in the cockpit of a North American T-6 Texan plane. *Rod Lewllen (nephew) and Atterbury-Bakalar Museum*.

A Columbus, Indiana native, she was born on November 14, 1912, and graduated from Columbus High School in 1929. She earned her civilian pilot's license while she was attending the State College of Washington, where she graduated in 1933. In 1940, she married Edward Norbeck.[401]

The Norbecks were living in Honolulu on December 7, 1941, and after the attack, they volunteered to become air wardens. When Edward joined the army in 1943, Jeanne, wanting to do her part, joined the Women Airforce Service Pilots (WASPs) that same year.[402] After completing her training, she was assigned as a test pilot at Camp Shaw in South Carolina. She and other WASPs flew training planes that had been red lined due to mechanical problems.[403] On October 16, 1944, she was assigned to test-fly a Vultee BT-13 primary trainer that had been reported as having a stuck wing. During her flight, the left wing failed, and she crashed while attempting to land. Norbeck was killed instantly.[404] Her body was transported back to her hometown in Columbus, where she received a burial that included a flag and military escort, an unusual honor because WASPs were listed as civil service employees and not official members of the military.[405] She was thirty-two years old at the time of her death. She and Edward had no children. The local hero's service was later memorialized with the naming of the chapel at the former Atterbury Air Base.

Both the museum and the chapel help keep alive the memory of those who served in the U.S. Army Air Forces at Atterbury Army Air Field during World War II.

For more information, visit https://www.atterburybakalarairmuseum.org.

PART III

SOUTHERN INDIANA

21

INDIANA MILITARY MUSEUM

Vincennes is Indiana's oldest town. Founded by French fur traders in 1772, it is a city known for its jewels of Hoosier history. Sitting along the Wabash River in southwest Indiana, the city was once the site of Fort Vincennes and the battle won by George Rogers Clark and his men as they defeated the British in 1779. The George Rogers Clark Memorial commemorates the man and the victory in the cause for freedom. The town also became the first capital for the Indiana Territory in 1800. Historic buildings from that era are prime tourist sites.

In 1984, the city welcomed the Indiana Military Museum (IMM) as another great attraction to celebrate Indiana history and the cause for freedom. The museum came into existence through the leadership of Knox County Superior Court judge Jim R. Osborne, who had been a collector of military artifacts for many years. Osborne, a Vincennes native, is both chairman of the museum's board and its curator.

Osborne's interest in history, especially that of World War II, began early in his life. At the age of five, he watched many John Wayne World War II movies at one of the drive-in theaters his father had built. When Osborne was seven years old, a neighbor across the street, a World War II veteran, was getting ready to place in the trash a box full of items he had brought home from the war, including a German helmet and flag. Osborne was outside at the time, watching him. When the neighbor noticed his interest, he asked the young boy if he would like the box of war memorabilia. "That was the collection starting to mushroom, right there at seven years old," Osborne said in a video segment posted on the museum's website.[406]

Throughout his school years, Osborne continued to collect military items, storing them in his parents' basement and garage. Military vehicles he acquired were parked in his parents' yard. His first artillery piece, a cannon, once sat in the front of a farmer's driveway. Osborne visited the piece so often that the farmer eventually gave it to him.[407]

Osborne earned a history degree from Vincennes University and Indiana University and then taught the subject for four years, often bringing pieces of his collection into class to show his students. After his short stint as a teacher, he returned to academia and pursued a law degree at Indiana University School of Law, graduating in 1974. He returned to Vincennes and started his law practice, which soon turned into an appointment as the first judge of the Knox County Court. His successful career provided him the income for traveling to war sites in Europe and buying military artifacts.[408]

In the early 1980s, people began suggesting to Osborne that he turn his private collection into a museum. He embraced the idea. In 1982, he and interested friends formed a not-for-profit museum corporation and began planning for a future museum in Vincennes. The original museum was housed in a building on two acres off Old Bruceville Road, two miles east of the city. It remained there for twenty-five years.

Continued growth in Osborne's collection necessitated a relocation to larger property and facilities. In the summer of 2012, the museum moved to a fourteen-acre site next to the Vincennes/Knox County Convention and Visitors Bureau on 715 South Sixth Street and celebrated a grand opening in May 2013. The site included a six-thousand-square-foot exhibition center and a large warehouse for storage. In 2019, the eight-thousand-square-foot warehouse was renovated to display new exhibits.[409]

Inside the renovated warehouse, which has now become the Museum Annex, are ten life-size diorama exhibits that immerse visitors in the combat experiences from World War I to the present. The World War II dioramas, taking up the largest portion of the annex, transport visitors back to the 1940s and feature life at home and in the European and Pacific Theaters of the war. The American Homefront exhibits include cutaway views inside a typical 1941 home. There is also a manufacturing exhibit showing the importance of war production and the vital role of women making war products. Rosie the Riveter mannequins appear to be making plane parts with authentic lathes and drill presses. A World War II barracks cutaway

Paratrooper descending in front of the cathedral at the European Theater Exhibit. *Ronald May.*

brings the war closer to home and gives visitors a glimpse of the military training environment for the men and women who prepared for war.

The European Theater diorama features an eighty-foot-long replica wall of a bombed-out Gothic cathedral. Formerly constructed for a Hollywood movie set, the cathedral backdrop now conveys the war in Normandy. The façade includes broken stained-glass windows and pock-holes from bullets and mortars hitting the stone block. Fifteen U.S., British and German vehicles and tanks, as well as artillery pieces, are lined along both walls of the church. Above the exhibit, U.S. paratroopers are shown descending into the battle. Adding to the experience are recorded sounds of military planes that accompany moving shadows on the floor, which mimic planes passing overhead, all of which gives a realistic feel to the combat setting.[410]

Equally impressive is the Pacific Theater exhibit, which includes an authentic Landing Craft Vehicle Personnel (LCVP), also known as a "Higgins Boat," that carried troops from the ships to the shore. One of twelve known LCVP's to exist in the world, the display shows the ramp down and allows the visitor to see the inside of the craft, which could hold twenty-five to thirty men. Above the LCVP is a gray wall conveying the side hull of a large ship. It has mannequin soldiers dressed in combat gear climbing down the netting toward the LCVP below them. This disembarking process was repeated dozens of times in the Pacific Theater as Allied forces leap-frogged from island to island in their combat path toward Japan. Completing the

Japanese Theater exhibit with U.S. marines and a Japanese tank, Indiana Military Museum. *Ronald May.*

Pacific Theater exhibits are U.S. and Japanese tanks and artillery, along with soldier mannequins in uniform, set in a re-created jungle combat scene and beach landing environment.[411]

On the grounds outside the Museum Annex, visitors will find a re-created concrete German bunker from the Second World War, as well as tracked and amphibious vehicles, many of them from World War II. These include an amphibious Landing Vehicle Tracked (LVT-4) and a six-wheel amphibious vehicle referred to as a "Duck" (DUKW). There are also several World War II planes on display. Stretching their proud wings are a C-47 and C-45 cargo plane, among other war-era aircraft.

Greeting visitors at the entrance to the museum's exhibit building is a torpedo display from the USS *Grayback* submarine (SS 208, the "Gray Ghost"), which was lost at sea between Luzon and Formosa in February 1944 while on its tenth patrol.

Inside the museum's exhibit center, glass-encased displays and free-standing artifacts are arranged chronologically from the Revolutionary War to the more recent war in Afghanistan. The armor collection inside the exhibit center includes the popular U.S. Sherman tank, as well as a German half-track and a Japanese light tank.

The World War II section of the exhibit center includes an authentic certified and serial numbered piece of steel from the USS *Arizona* battleship, which was sunk by the Japanese in their attack at Pearl Harbor. In the display commemorating D-Day are jump jackets worn by the paratroopers, along with field equipment. General Eisenhower's full Class A uniform, which was tailored in London a few days before D-Day; General Patton's tanker's jacket; and General Mark Clark's uniform can also be found in this section.

In the Pacific War display, visitors can view Japanese tanks and see some of the black volcanic ash/sand from Iwo Jima, where so many marines bled and died to secure the island and raise the U.S. flag. Even some Ground Zero objects from the bombed city of Hiroshima, Japan, are on display, along with other end-of-the-war artifacts.

Red Skelton. *Red Skelton Museum of American Comedy.*

Most of the other World War II display cases are used to present the personal service stories and artifacts of local Vincennes and Knox County veterans. Among those is the display of favorite hometown son and beloved Hoosier entertainer Richard (Red) Skelton. The museum has one of his military uniforms and other memorabilia. Born in 1913 in Vincennes, Skelton got an early start in the entertainment business as a teenager appearing in a circus. At the age of fifteen, he was on the road full time, working a circuit of entertainment venues. By 1941, he had his own radio show and had become a household name. He used his fame and his shows to help sell war bonds after the United States entered World War II.[412]

In March 1944, Skelton was drafted into the army, and his radio show was discontinued. Although content to serve as an infantryman, he was soon assigned to an army entertainment unit as a performing arts specialist. Following his training at the Washington and Lee College, Army Special Service School, he performed shows for troops in Virginia and New Jersey, often twelve a day. In April 1945, he was shipped overseas to entertain army units at Camp Darby in Italy. One month later, Skelton suffered a nervous breakdown, possibly due to the exhaustive number of shows he was performing. He spent the remainder of the war in a hospital at Camp Pickett, Virginia, and was honorably discharged in September that year.[413]

In December 1945, Skelton resumed his radio show and acting career, which continued until 1993. In addition to acting, he also became an accomplished painter of clowns.[414] The IMM has a few of his original clown paintings on display. Skelton enjoyed a seventy-year run in show business before he died in 1997 at the age of eighty-four. Today, his life and career as an entertainer are preserved in the Red Skelton Museum of American Comedy at Vincennes.

Adding much to the museum's appeal and educational value is an extensive outdoor area behind the museum exhibit building that has been converted into a battlefield and used for hosting living history events since 2008. Several times a year, military reenactors come from all around the Midwest to set up camps with displays of authentic era equipment and re-create battles from World War I, World War II, Korea and Vietnam, often using some of the museum's vehicles. The weekend events pay tribute to the veterans who fought in each war.

A five-year-old boy's interest in World War II, which turned into a young man's dream for a museum has, over the years, blossomed into a world-class military museum for Vincennes. The IMM today is one of the most outstanding and comprehensive U.S. military history and educational facilities in the Midwest. It houses more than 100,000 artifacts and enjoys thousands of visitors each year, attracting guests from all over the nation and many foreign countries. This newest jewel in Vincennes's crown is well worth the trip.[415]

For more information, visit the museum's website at www.indianamilitarymuseum.org.

22

NAVAL AMMUNITION DEPOT

The third-largest U.S. Navy installation in the world isn't anywhere near an ocean. Rather, it is in the remote, largely unpopulated and rural stretches of Martin County in southern Indiana. In the mid-1930s, the federal government purchased thirty-two thousand acres of submarginal land unsuitable for agriculture in northern Martin County to use for conservation. The plan was to repurpose the land through reforestation, recreation and a wildlife preserve and then lease it back to the State of Indiana. That plan changed with the advent of the Second World War.[416]

By October 1940, local newspapers reported that the Navy Department was considering the state-owned land for the construction of a large depot to store ammunition for their Atlantic fleet of ships.[417] The navy had been looking for several years for an inland ammunition depot west of the Appalachian Mountains.[418] Federal money was made available for such a purchase in 1940. The northern part of Martin County, Indiana, proved to be the ideal location. Its inland location, far from the East Coast, protected it from the threat of enemy submarine or airborne bombardment. A large portion of land with low market value was already state owned. The land was far from cities and population centers, but it still had decent road and railway access for shipping, as well as a water supply and power. And its hilly, forested terrain allowed for excellent concealment of the storage magazines.[419]

Navy officials announced that the mission of the new depot was to "store, prepare, and issue all types of ammunition and maintain and operate various types of ammunition loading and processing plants. Plans called for

Navy Ammunition Depot Crane, Administration Building 1. *Ronald May.*

the erection of a hundred or more smokeless powder magazines, storage warehouses, shop buildings, barracks, homes for Navy officers, administrative buildings, etc."[420]

Construction of the new depot began in January 1941. It was commissioned on December 1, 1941, six days before the Japanese attack at Pearl Harbor.[421] The depot was officially named the Naval Ammunition Depot, Burns City, but in 1943, it was renamed the U.S. Naval Ammunition Depot Crane, Indiana (NAD Crane), to honor Commodore William Montgomery Crane of New Jersey. He was the first chief of the Bureau of Ordnance and Hydrography for the navy in 1842. A limestone bust of the commodore was placed across the street from the base's first structure, the Administration Building (Building 1), and both are still there today.[422]

The United States' entrance into the war brought an increased fervor to the construction and production demands on the depot. Another thirty-two thousand acres were purchased by the government, bringing the total land usage for the Navy Ammunition Depot to sixty-four thousand acres. While most of the ammunition depot remained in Martin County, portions of it were also in Greene and Lawrence Counties.[423] Many of the famers forced off the land by the ever-growing depot's reaches were eventually hired to work at Crane.[424]

Navy Ammunition Depot Crane, earth-covered ammo storage. *Ronald May.*

Some of the most significant structures built on the depot included "1,054 arch-type magazines, 510 inflammable materials magazines, 167 inert storehouses, five torpedo storehouses, 138 miles of railroad, 226 miles of roads, 65 miles of water lines, and production facilities for small-projectile and flare-loading, mine and bomb filling, case preparation, rocket motor assembly, and 20- and 40-mm. ammunition manufacture."[425]

One of the most important and costly buildings on the depot was the pyrotechnic or star shell plant. "Parachutes were attached to them, and when they were dropped behind the enemy lines, they descended slowly and illuminated enemy targets."[426] Their worth was affirmed in a telegram to NAD Crane from Rear Admiral W.H.P. Blandy, chief of the Bureau Ordnance:

> *Parachute flares such as you manufacture for the Navy have proven to be an important factor in the success of night bombing missions. The Commanding Officer of a Patrol Squadron who took part in the first air raid on Munda reported: "On night attacks we always pull flares as we finish our bombing run. We think these flares are wonderful things to help in the get-a-way. They are so bright and blinding that any anti-aircraft fire is usually thrown off completely by them." You are to be congratulated on producing equipment of such value to our gallant Naval Aviators.[427]*

Crane navy employees working on a munitions production line in 1942. *U.S. Army.*

The navy initially projected that Crane would need 500 to 750 civilians to work at the ammunition depot. Once the United States entered the war, that number increased dramatically.[428] The depot quickly faced significant labor shortages with young men getting drafted or enlisting for military service. The diminished labor pool was augmented by employing teen boys, referred to as BOWs (Boy Ordnance Workers), and young women, known as WOWs (Women Ordnance Workers), many of them under the age of eighteen.[429]

Raymond Thornton Thomas was one of the BOWs at NAD Crane. The Martin County native was born in 1927 and lived with his parents and seven siblings on a rented farm near Burns City. In 1941, the government bought the farm they were renting to expand the Navy Ammunition Depot footprint. The family relocated to Linton, Indiana. In January 1944, Thomas dropped out of high school and accepted a job at NAD Crane. He had just turned sixteen. He was placed on a crew that loaded bombs for overseas shipment. "I worked in TNT and all kinds of explosives," he said during a 1991 University of Southern Indiana oral history interview with Thomas Rogers. "There was yellow powder—Comp D. It was pretty hard work."[430]

Thomas worked at Crane two years before getting drafted into the army in December 1945. Following his eighteen months of military service, most of it spent in Italy, he returned to NAD Crane and worked for another twenty-eight years, mostly hauling explosives on tractor trailers to storage locations on the base. "We would haul them to the field buildings," he recalled during his interview. "They had thousands of those buildings out there. You could haul for days, months, years, and not get them full."[431]

Lucille Arvin of Martin County was one of the first women employed at the base. In July 1942, she began working in the production-ammunition loading plant. She was taught how to "safely explosive load, press, fuze, paint, mark, inspect, and pack for shipment to the fleet."[432] By October 1944, women were doing even more of the work once done by the men. "By then men were very scarce," recalled Arvin. "Women had to do all operations: loading and unloading boxcars and some trucks; some truck drivers were women; opening boxes of component parts; palletizing loaded rockets; and assisting with testing on the Rocket Range."[433]

Even with these efforts, there were still labor shortages. In 1944, the navy employed 200 Indiana University students to work on weekends. In March of the same year, a detachment of WAVES (Women Accepted for Volunteer Emergency Service) arrived, and in August, the navy established an Ordnance Battalion that consisted of 1,200 Navy Seabees.[434]

The number of civilian employees at NAD Crane had climbed to 9,500 by the summer of 1945. The flow of workers came from one hundred different towns and villages, and some of them traveled distances of 140 miles roundtrip. More than a third of the close to 10,000 workers were women.[435]

The workers, both civilian and military, proved effective in their output. During the months of August to October 1944, the monthly production average was fifty thousand tons of shells, flares and other munitions being shipped out for war.[436] Added to this impressive number of munitions were some of the first rockets used in the war. They "were transported to Indianapolis in armed trucks and then flown to both coasts for aerial transportation to the fighting fronts. Records show that in some instances they were fired at the enemy within four days after leaving the depot."[437]

Reflecting on his early years at Crane, Ralph E. Graves, who helped construct the base and then became a lifetime employee, said this of the depot: "World War II was an exciting time because people were coming and going at a high rate. And they would bring back stories of how our ammunition was working."[438]

As it turned out, the ammunition worked well enough not only to help win the war but also to ensure the navy's presence in rural southern Indiana for generations to come. By January 1945, the Navy Department had decided to expand the operations at NAD Crane at a cost of $10 million.[439] Today, the depot is called the Naval Surface Warfare Center, Crane Division. It is the principal tenant command located at Naval Support Activity Crane (NSA Crane) and employs more than 3,800 people. Its mission is to "provide acquisition engineering, in-service engineering and technical support for sensors, electronics, electronic warfare, and special warfare weapons."[440] And it remains the third-largest navy installation in the world and a major employer in rural Martin and surrounding counties.

23

FREEMAN ARMY AIRFIELD AND MUSEUM

On December 1, 1942, almost one year after the Japanese attack at Pearl Harbor, another military airfield appeared on Indiana soil. This one was located near the South Central Indiana town of Seymour.

In April 1942, Lieutenant Colonel Preuss of the U.S. Army Air Corps made an official visit to Seymour to consider the site for a potential new airfield. Like the other airfields dotting the Indiana landscape, the rural site was chosen largely because of its proximity to major transportation arteries: the Baltimore, Ohio and Pennsylvania Railroad lines and U.S. Highways 31 and 50. The Seymour location was perhaps also selected because Lieutenant Colonel Preuss was a native of Seymour.[441]

Construction of the airfield began in May 1942 and was completed nine months later in February 1943 at a cost of more than $1 million. When it was finished, four paved runways, more than four hundred buildings and twelve miles of road replaced twenty-seven farms on 2,600 acres and transformed the once tranquil agricultural setting into a little city with a beehive of military activity.[442]

Freeman Army Airfield was built to train U.S. Army Air Forces pilots to fly multi-engine planes. Having already completed their preflight, primary and basic schools, the pilots who reported to Freeman Field were introduced to twin-engine planes in preparation for flying bombers or transport aircraft in combat theaters. Pilot trainees flew one of 250 Beech AT-10 "Wichita" aircraft throughout the nine-week course. The AT-10s were twin-engine training planes composed mostly of wood. Following their graduation, the

Freeman Field, Foreign Aircraft Evaluation Center. *Freeman Army Airfield Museum.*

pilots proceeded to their final phase of training at a different base to learn to fly the specific bomber or transport plane to which they were assigned.[443]

Among the four hundred buildings on the base, five of them housed Link Trainers, twelve in each building.[444] The Link Trainers, developed by Edward Link in 1929, were the first generation of flight simulators that taught cadets how to fly by instrument reading and radio navigation. The simulator instructors, often women, monitored the simulation with equipment on a nearby desk connected to the simulator's sensors by cables. The student's flight path was accurately traced by an Automatic Recorder. More than 500,000 U.S. aviation cadets were trained on such simulators during World War II and the Korean Conflict.[445]

The first class of 121 pilots graduated from the new airfield on April 29, 1943. This was also the occasion for the renaming of the airfield. Initially called the Army Air Base, Seymour, the name was changed to Freeman Army Airfield to honor Captain Richard Freeman of Winamac, Indiana. Freeman was a West Point graduate who was killed in 1941 when his plane, an experimental version of the B-17 bomber, crashed in Nevada during a training exercise and killed all eight crewmen.[446]

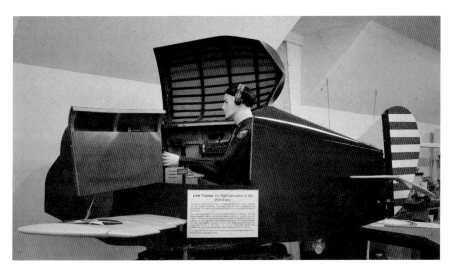

Link Trainer at Freeman Army Airfield Museum. *Ronald May*.

Ken McKain, *at left, standing*; AT-10 is in the background. *Freeman Army Airfield Museum*.

The only Seymour-area native to receive his training at Freeman Airfield was Lieutenant William Kenneth (Ken) McKain. Born in 1916, he joined the U.S. Army Air Corps in January 1941 and served in Panama at an air depot. While returning to the United States to begin pilot training in 1942, his ship was torpedoed by a German submarine. He and several other survivors were rescued from their lifeboat twelve hours later by a navy vessel in the area.[447]

After completing his primary pilot training, McKain reported to Freeman Field and graduated with Class 43-I on October 1, 1943. Following the graduation ceremony, he married Alma Mann in the base chapel.[448] He served as a copilot and later as the first pilot of a B-24 in the 459th Bomb Group, 15th Air Force. The bomber was named the "Satan Shuttlebus" and sported on the plane nose a painted caricature of Hitler with an arrow piercing his heart. McKain flew fifty missions in southern Europe, bombing enemy targets in Munich, Vienna, France, Romania, Yugoslavia and cities in North Italy. He was one of only two original pilots of the 459th Group who remained in the group when the war ended, the others having been killed or taken as POWs. After returning to the United States in September 1944, McKain became a flight instructor at Victorville Army Airfield in Victorville, California. On May 4, 1945, four days before Germany surrendered, he died in an accident while flying a B-29 Superfortress in a night training exercise over California.[449]

A total of nineteen classes, consisting of 4,245 pilots, graduated from the twin-engine training at Freeman Army Airfield from April 1943 to February 1945. Tragically, 23 of the cadet pilots lost their lives during the training. At the peak of military operations, there were more than 5,000 men and women stationed at Freeman, including Women Airforce Service Pilots (WASP), who ferried planes to the base and tested malfunctioning planes after their engines were rebuilt.[450] Most of the pilots who graduated from Freeman Army Airfield were assigned to the 8th Air Force in England for duty in the European Theater.[451]

In April 1945, an incident occurred on base that attracted national attention. It became known as the "Freeman Field Mutiny." That spring, two squadrons of the newly formed 477th Bombardment Group arrived at Freeman Field to continue training for B-25J bombers. Both squadrons were made up of African American men who had been selected for the "Tuskegee experiment," the training of Black pilots and crew for service in the U.S. Army Air Forces. Although many of the first Tuskegee pilots were trained as fighter pilots—they became known as "Red Tails" for the red tail on the

P-51 Mustangs they flew—others were tagged for flying bombers. The two bomber squadrons that reported to Freeman Field, the 616th and 617th, consisted of one hundred crewmen.[452]

Shortly after arriving on base, a small group of the Black flight officers went into the all-white officers' club, which had been made off-limits to them by the illegal action of the base commander, Colonel Richard Selway. The presence of Black men in a white men's club created a stir. When a group of Black officers tried to return to the club the next day, they were barred from entering and arrested by the provost marshal.[453]

Connie Nappier Jr. was among the Tuskegee group at Freeman Field. Born in Georgia, he grew up in Hartford, Connecticut, and enlisted in the U.S. Army Air Forces in 1943. He was assigned as a bombardier navigator in the 616th Squadron, which came to Freeman Army Airfield in Seymour in April 1945.[454]

Although Nappier was not among those who had entered the white officers' club—in fact, most of the 101 men in the two squadrons never entered it—he and the other Black crewmen were "guilty" because they shared the same skin color as those who did enter the club.

The interim commanding officer of the base, Colonel Selway, drew up an agreement in writing pledging acceptance of the segregation requirements. He insisted that all the 101 Black men of the two squadrons sign the agreement. "He ordered us to sign," recalled Nappier in an interview for the Library of Congress's Veterans History Project, "which was tantamount to our agreeing to segregate ourselves. And we said, 'No'—knowing full well what the outcome could be." (Disobedience of a lawful order under the Articles of War can result in death.) "Well, we knew that," acknowledged Nappier, "but fellows said, 'Hey, we could go overseas and die. We might as well die here for what we know is right.'" Subsequently, after refusing to sign the agreement, all 101 Black officers of the two squadrons were arrested, confined to their barracks and scheduled for a court-martial.[455]

The men were transported to Godman Field in Kentucky and placed in the stockades while awaiting general court-martial. They were later released by order of Army Chief of Staff General George Marshall. Instead of being sent to the combat theater, the two squadrons were assigned to Walterboro, South Carolina, to patrol the coast and search for German U-boats in their B-25 bombers. Many of the men thought that their new assignment was also a form of discrimination, keeping them from serving overseas in combat.[456]

The Freeman Field Mutiny resulted in some bad press for the U.S. Army Air Forces. The peaceful protest of the Tuskegee Airmen was one of the contributing factors that motivated President Harry Truman to issue an executive order in 1948 officially ending segregation in the U.S. Armed Forces.[457]

After the war in Europe concluded, Freeman Field was designated a Foreign Aircraft Evaluation Center in June 1945. During the next fourteen months, 160 enemy German, Japanese and Italian aircraft were shipped to the airfield for analysis.[458] German aircraft mechanic prisoners of war interned at nearby Camp Atterbury were shuttled to the airfield to help assemble the German planes.[459] Among the inventory of foreign aircraft was the German ME-262, the first fighter jet used in the war, as well as the V-1 and V-2 rockets. When the base closed in October 1946, most of the planes were sent to the Smithsonian, Wright-Patterson Air Force Base in Dayton, Ohio, or Davis Mothan Air Force Base in Arizona to be scrapped.[460]

During the period of foreign aircraft evaluation, Freeman Field also became home, briefly, to the first army helicopter training for the Sikorsky R4 "Hoverfly."[461] The helicopter was used for observation and ferrying supplies in the European Theater and, at the end of the war, in the China-Burma-India Theater for rescue operations.[462] The helicopter training at Freeman lasted only three months before the program was transferred to Chanute Army Airfield in Illinois.[463]

At the end of 1945, the U.S. Army Air Forces glider branch and flight test and engineering operations moved to Freeman Field. It remained there until March 1946, when the training relocated to Wilmington, Ohio.[464]

In 1947, following the closing of the airfield, the government gave the property to the City of Seymour with the understanding that it would always use it for an airport. Today, the Freeman Municipal Airport in Seymour occupies part of the former airfield. About 1,500 other acres are rented to local farmers. The remainder of the former government property includes an industrial park with sixty businesses.[465]

The Freeman Army Airfield Museum occupies two of the original base buildings. Started in 1996 by some dedicated area residents, the museum preserves the history of the airfield and the cadets who trained there during World War II. Displays for the museum came largely from donations of former cadets who trained there or from families of cadets. The museum is housed in two former three-thousand-square-foot Link Trainer buildings used during the war. The first building contains items related to the history of the base, information on the cadets, models of the various bombers along

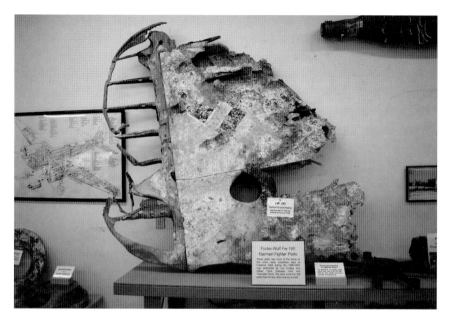

Focke-Wulf Fw-190 vertical fin and rudder, Freeman Army Airfield Museum Annex. *Ronald May.*

with actual bombs, some weapons, a mockup War Room, a Tuskegee Airmen exhibit, an exhibit of women who served during the war and displays of uniforms and equipment. The second building, referred to as the Museum Annex, houses larger items, including a Link Trainer, a restored World War II–era fire truck that served the base, aircraft engine and propellers from Allied aircraft and parts from foreign planes that were examined following the war when Freeman Field became a Foreign Aircraft Evaluation Center.[466]

Freeman Army Airfield has a proud and diverse history of service during World War II. Visitors to the museum will be glad they stopped to review the legacy of Seymour's contribution to the war effort.

For more information, visit https://freemanarmyairfieldmuseum.org.

24

JEFFERSON PROVING GROUND

T hose living in rural Jefferson, Jennings and Ripley Counties in southeastern Indiana know when hunting season begins as they hear the crack of rifles and boom of shotguns. On May 12, 1941, the first of a very different kind of ammunition, a .50-caliber round, was fired and heard by people living as far away as Madison, more than ten miles south.[467] It was the dawn of a new era and changed the lives and landscape of the people living in southeastern Indiana.

Officially, the eighty-six-square-mile property became the Jefferson Proving Ground, but soon people started referring to it simply as "JPG." The heavily wooded region that encompassed more than fifty-five thousand acres in three counties was, prior to 1941, home to 500 families, many small farms, 5 villages, 6 churches, 4 schools and 21 cemeteries.[468] All of them were moved or abandoned by order of the federal government to make room for an ammunition testing ground that was to include 120 buildings, an airport and thousands of acres designated as firing ranges for testing rounds of ammunition.[469]

Prior to 1940, the Aberdeen Testing Ground in Maryland was the only place where ammunition for the army was tested. But with war looming in Europe and Southeast Asia, the army needed a newer and larger site to test its projectiles. Southeast Indiana was chosen in November 1940 as the most favorable location. Railway lines, federal highways and proximity to Charlestown, the location of a new ordnance manufacturing plant, made it the logical choice. The designated boundary for the fan-shaped proving

Jefferson Proving Ground, HQ Building. *Ronald May*.

Louis Munier and Jefferson Proving Ground exhibit, Jefferson County Historical Society Museum. *Ronald May*.

ground stretched north for seventeen and a half miles. It was three miles wide at the south end and six miles wide on the north end.[470]

Following the official announcement in December 1940, the government moved quickly to purchase the land for $3 million through eminent domain proceedings.[471] Residents within the proving ground boundaries were informed that they had to vacate their homes, many of them having only thirty days to do so once the sale was finalized.[472]

Charles Louis Munier, a Jefferson County native born in 1919, grew up in one of those homes. Although his family had already relocated before the government purchased the property, the home where four generations of Muniers had once lived was still owned by the family before becoming part of the proving ground.

Munier served two years in the army before being medically discharged. Returning home, he found a job repairing artillery pieces at JPG. "I worked on all the guns that they were testing on the firing line," he shared in a 2006 interview with Mike Moore. "After a while there, they gave me the job of ordering the gun parts."[473]

Munier had the rare experience of seeing his childhood home four years after it had become part of JPG. On July 4, 1945, he was asked to go fishing on Big Creek with Captain May, who was a supervisor of the firing line. "He took me out there where I lived," said Munier. "Our house was still there, about like it was before the government took over the farm. The back part of the house was stone. I went up there on the second floor and looked in the room where my sisters lived. There was a 75mm projectile lying there on the floor, it knocked a hole on that back wall…so I got out of there fast. I don't think the Army used it for target practice, I think it just landed there."[474]

The 75mm projectiles were not the only rounds littering the landscape. Millions of different projectiles landed on the ground at JPG, evidence of its mission to test army ammunition from 20mm aircraft canons up to 155mm and 240mm field guns.[475] The ordnance list also included bombs, mines, rockets, flares and signals.[476] The tests were to determine if the powder manufactured by the Charlestown munition plant, forty-five miles south of JPG, met the specifications required by the army.[477]

Every component of ammunition that made up a round was tested individually and collectively: cartridge case, primer, propelling charge, projectile or bullet, the bursting charge or explosive and the fuse.[478] JPG had thirty-two firing points for testing ammunition. There were also nineteen recovery fields for retrieving projectiles for further examination. The fields were anywhere from five hundred yards to sixteen thousand yards (nine

M204 105mm Howitzer firing test at Jefferson Proving Ground. *Jefferson County Historical Society.*

miles) from the firing line, depending on the projectile fired and the weapon used to fire it. Each field had a bombproof shelter where two observers were assigned to evaluate the timing and results of the expelled ammunition, as well as the performance of the powder used.[479]

Staff correspondent Bill Ladd of Louisville's *Courier-Journal* described the testing process in his November 2, 1941 column: "It seems that powder manufactured at a powder mill differs occasionally in strength. At a proving ground they line up numerous guns and fire actual projectiles. First, they fire with a shell with standard powder. Then they fire with the latest lot from the powder mill. A bevy of unfortunate guys are posted at approximately the spot where the shell is expected to land. They are protected amply by bombproof shelters. The second shell lands, these men telephone back to officials a comparison of the results of the standard powder and the new lot."[480]

The job as an observer was not without danger, as Charles Keith Stewart found out. Stewart was a civilian aerial observer at JPG from November 1941 to December 1942. He wrote about one experience in early 1942 while he was positioned at an abandoned house used as an aerial target:

On this particular run when the three bombs dropped, one veered slightly down from the other two. Of course, I followed the flight of the two rather than the one which left my field of view. I was standing where the walls were waist high or slightly more—the men with me had crouched at the time of the drop. The airplane speed was about 150 miles per hour so that the bombs at that low altitude had more forward motion than drop. As the bombs got close, I saw that they would be slightly west and a little high of the house—and suddenly thought, "Where is the other one?" Instantly I dropped to the ground and, a fraction of a second later, the bomb struck the wall directly behind me. Had I remained standing, it would have struck me around the chest and torn me in two.[481]

Flying one of the B-25 planes during that day's testing was a little-known lieutenant by the name of Charles W. Sweeney, who was born in 1919 and hailed from Lowell, Massachusetts. Following his commissioning as a second lieutenant on December 12, 1941, Sweeney was assigned to an Army Air Corps detachment of pilots designated to fly bombers and fighter planes at JPG, which had built a six-mile-square airport on its grounds to accommodate even the largest bombers for testing ammunition drops.[482]

Sweeney was a bit of a daredevil who enjoyed occasionally flying under the Madison Milton Bridge, even though orders prohibited it. He had his own experience with a mishap one day when his bombardier dropped eight five-hundred-pound bombs from the plane. The bombs missed their intended mark and landed outside the boundary of the proving ground in a farm field near the town of Nebraska. Thankfully, the bombs had not been armed, and no one was hurt. Despite the efforts of four hundred men to locate the unexploded ordnance, they were never found and remain today submerged in the soil somewhere.[483] The mishap notwithstanding, it was a different kind of bomb drop three and a half years later that sealed Sweeney's place in military history.

While he enjoyed his time at JPG, Sweeney wanted to fly in combat. He asked for a transfer to Eglin Field Military Reservation in Florida (today Eglin Air Force Base), where he met Colonel Paul Tibbets and joined his unit of B-29 bombers.[484] On August 6, 1945, Sweeney flew with Tibbets's group in a different bomber as Tibbets dropped the first atomic bomb from the *Enola Gay* on the city of Hiroshima. Three days later, on August 9, Sweeney flew the B-29 named *Bockscar*, which dropped the second atomic bomb, this one on Nagasaki. He barely had enough fuel to make it back to the island of Tinian. Japan surrendered eight days later.[485]

The Jefferson Proving Ground "proved" itself worthy in every way during its World War II operations. On September 8, 1942, JPG received the Army-Navy "E" Pennant for its production and efficiency.[486] At its peak of operations, there were 1,200 employees, almost a quarter of whom were women.[487] Safety measures also proved effective. During its fifty-plus years of operation, only 2 workers lost their lives in accidents.[488]

Of all the projectiles fired, it was never the ammunition itself but rather a simple piece of paper labeled "Test Report" that proved to be the most important contribution of the proving ground: "Nothing fancy and yet this plain bureaucratic report saved thousands of American and Allied lives.… The test report was the final outcome of testing. Either the munitions performed according to specifications, and they were accepted, or they didn't and were not. There are stories of pallets of ammunition being pushed overboard from transport ships headed towards Europe during World War II, Korea, and Vietnam because the randomly selected lot of munitions sent to JPG did not pass the test. Imagine the possible consequences had our servicemen used bad ammunition."[489] It was the job of JPG to make sure the ammunition used by American soldiers was safe and performed according to army specifications.

In 1995, the U.S. government closed Jefferson Proving Ground. Most of the equipment and operation was relocated to the Yuma, Arizona Proving Ground.[490] During its fifty-three years of operation, "approximately 24 million rounds were fired, and it is estimated that a million and a half are 'duds'—those rounds that did not go off but still pose a potential hazard."[491] Some thirty thousand acres remain fenced off today to guard the public from the danger of the unexploded ordnance.[492]

In 2000, five years after the installation closed, the north section of the proving ground was designated as the Big Oaks National Wildlife Refuge.[493]

When operations first began, JPG officials stated that the test firing would be little noticed by the residents of nearby Madison. They believed that Madison's distance away (ten miles) and drop in elevation would ensure that residents there would hear only muffled sounds from the test firing.[494] That Madison residents soon referred to their city as "Boomtown" suggests otherwise.[495] In the end, the annoying and less-than-muffled sounds of ammunition fired at JPG during the years of World War II were ultimately the sounds ensuring safe and accurate ammunition for the cause of freedom. Today, the sounds most prevalent at the former testing ground are the sounds of returning wildlife and nature reclaiming her now peaceful home.

25

EVANSVILLE WARTIME MUSEUM

No city in the state of Indiana contributed more to war materiél production during World War II than Evansville. Located at the southern tip of Indiana along the Ohio River, this industrial city produced, among other things, bullets, tanks, vehicles, ships and planes. Overall production levels reached astounding levels in many of the eighty-plus factories that contributed to the war effort:[496]

- 3.2 billion rounds of .45-caliber ammunition
- 20 million 40mm shell casings
- 9 million 37mm shell casings
- 6,670 Republic P-47 Thunderbolt fighter aircraft
- 4,000 army trucks rebuilt
- 1,662 Sherman Tanks reconditioned
- 167 Landing Ships, Tank (LSTs)
- $150 million in war bonds and stamps purchased[497]

The story of the city's World War II legacy is presented well at the Evansville Wartime Museum (EWM). Located in a hangar at the west end of the Evansville Regional Airport at 7503 Petersburg Road, the museum opened in May 2017 after five years of planning.[498]

Following the United States entering World War II, the city of Evansville was transformed into a hub of production. Workers from Indiana counties near Evansville as well as nearby Illinois and Kentucky poured into the city to fill the available jobs, making Evansville one of the busiest industrial cities in the country.[199]

The EWM tells Evansville's story through several different galleries: Homefront, World War I, World War II and the Main Gallery. There is also a flight simulator room for those who wish to try their hand flying virtually.

The Homefront gallery's photos, information cards and displays tell the story of the diverse defense plants in Evansville that produced the things necessary for the war. There were eighty companies that were converted to wartime production. Fifteen of them earned the Army-Navy "E" Award for their work. The four largest companies—Chrysler Motor Plant, Evansville Shipyard, International Steel and Republic Aviation—all earned more than one "E" award.[500]

The Chrysler Motor Plant, renamed the Evansville Ordnance Plant, produced ammunition, both .30- and .45-caliber. An impressive 96 percent of all .45-caliber ammunition used by American soldiers was produced by Chrysler. In addition to bullets, the company also refurbished and rebuilt 5,662 Sherman tanks and military trucks.[501]

The Evansville Shipyard, the largest of the Midwest "Cornfield Shipyards," produced 167 Landing Ship, Tanks at the forty-five-acre site along the banks of the Ohio River. Almost twenty thousand workers were employed there, and at its peak of operation the shipyard was turning out one LST every sixty days. Much of the steel for the ships was supplied by International Steel in Evansville.[502]

Republic Aviation Plant built 6,670 P-47 Thunderbolt fighters. The five thousand workers, of whom half were women, reached a production level of assembling fourteen of the planes every day.[503] This output represented 43 percent of the 15,660 planes made, making it the most produced American fighter aircraft used in the war.[504]

Native Hoosier Fred Fehsenfeld flew one of those P-47s in Europe, perhaps one built in Evansville. Fehsenfeld was born on October 10, 1924, in Indianapolis. He graduated from Shortridge High School in 1941 and began an engineering degree at Purdue University. On his eighteenth birthday, October 10, 1942, Fehsenfeld shifted his focus from college studies to military service. He enlisted in the U.S. Army Air Corps and pursued becoming a fighter pilot.[505]

After completing flight training on the P-47 Thunderbolt, Fehsenfeld was assigned to the 9th Fighter Command, 354th Pioneer Mustang Fighter Group, the 353rd Squadron stationed in France. "The next weeks were spent strafing and bomb diving," he wrote in a long reflection of his service in

Above: Republic Aviation Plant. *Evansville Wartime Museum.*

Left: Fred Fehsenfeld service photo. *Fred Fehsenfeld family.*

2004. "We destroyed Tiger tanks, bridges, ammunition dumps, and trains. It was not unusual for us to fly 3 to 3½ hour missions, sometimes as many as three per day."[506]

Fehsenfeld's squadron provided aerial support during the Battle of the Bulge. "The weather broke up on Christmas Day 1944," he recalled, "and we flew three missions a day for seven straight days. And, with the courageous actions of our ground troops, we stopped the attack."[507]

At the end of the war, he was honorably discharged. He left the service having flown eighty-nine missions in Europe and earning the Air Medal with three silver clusters and a Silver Star.[508]

Following his discharge, Fehsenfeld resumed his mechanical engineering degree at Purdue University, got married and became a successful businessman. He led his father's Indianapolis-based business, Crystal Flash Petroleum, into an unprecedented period of growth. He died in 2018 at the age of ninety-four.[509]

Service members like him are honored in EWM's World War II Honor Gallery. The room is filled with photos, uniforms and memorabilia from Evansville's sons and daughters who served in the war. One display case includes a beautiful white wedding gown made from the silk of a parachute.

Evansville's Red Cross Canteen was a stopping point for many servicemen making their way to and from training along the railways. Volunteers served meals, drinks and snacks donated by the community and area businesses to 1,612,000 men and women in uniform. All races were welcome. Up to 3,500 were served on peak days.[510] The museum has re-created part of the canteen as one of its exhibits.

The main gallery, the open hangar, has the largest space and includes several signature pieces in the museum: a P-47 fighter-bomber, a Sherman tank and a LCVP (Higgins Boat), completing the air, land and sea triad.

The P-47 was built by Republic Aviation in 1945 and saw service in Europe with the 358th Fighter Group, 366th Fighter Squadron, 9th Air Force. It flew with the moniker "Tarheel Hal." The Evansville P-47 Foundation had been trying for twenty years to acquire one for the museum. "Hal" was purchased from a museum in Houston, Texas, for $3.5 million. Renamed "Hoosier Spirit II," it is one of only four operational P-47s known to exist today.[511] A 1940 Boeing Stearman biplane used for training pilots is also on display near the P-47.

Not far from the P-47 is the newest acquisition for the museum, a fully restored and operational 1943 Chrysler M4A4 Sherman tank. The tank was used by the British army and was on display at the Normandy Tank

P-47 Hoosier Spirit II at the Evansville Wartime Museum. *Ronald May.*

Museum in Catz, France. In 2016, the tank was sent to the United States. EWM acquired it in 2022 from the American G.I. Museum in College Station, Texas.[512]

On the far corner of the main gallery is a Landing Craft, Vehicle and Personnel (LVCP), commonly known as a Higgins Boat, on loan from the LST 325 Memorial Ship in Evansville. More than twenty-three thousand of these boats were manufactured to bring up to thirty combat troops or eight thousand pounds of cargo from the larger ships to the shore. Made mostly from wood, these ten-by-thirty-six-foot small landing crafts were essential in amphibious operations and in winning the war.[513]

There are also numerous military vehicles and some 1942 automobile models, the last year of production before the auto industry turned to military production. The 1942 Oldsmobile B44 "Sixty" is among the models on display.[514]

The Evansville Wartime Museum is not the only proof of Evansville's incredible contributions during World War II. The National Park Service recently designated the city as an American World War II Heritage City.[515] The program is managed by the Department of the Interior, which can designate one city from each state for the honor.[516]

This unique and informative museum should be on the list for anyone wanting to learn how one Hoosier city made such a difference in the war effort.

For more information, visit https://www.evansvillewartimemuseum.org.

26

USS LST 325 SHIP MEMORIAL

A piece of World War II navy history rests on the Ohio River in Evansville, Indiana. Floating on the murky brown water, the gray steel structure carries the designation "LST 325." LST, an acronym for Landing Ship, Tank, was one of the navy's amphibious cargo ships.

Following the British defeat at Dunkirk, France, in 1940, Prime Minister Winston Churchill appealed to the United States to design a large amphibious ship that could cross an ocean carrying both troops and vehicles and get close enough to shore to land them without harbor facilities. The British had designed some early versions of amphibious ships, but they were unable to mass-produce the number needed for a large-scale operation.[517] The LST was developed to meet those needs.

The ship, 328 feet long and 50 feet wide, was large enough to carry a crew of 117 officers and enlisted men and a complement of 163 landing troops.[518] The cavernous tank deck inside the cargo hold, its most distinctive feature, carried up to twenty Sherman tanks or thirty-nine light Stuart tanks or seventeen amtracs. Lighter vehicles like trucks and trailers were packed in tightly on the weather deck above the cargo hold. Smaller landing crafts, LCVPs, were hung on the sides of the ship by davits. On average, each LST carried seventy military vehicles to an invasion beach.[519]

Based on a design by naval architect John C. Neidermair, who worked for the navy's Bureau of Ships, the LST was made with a flat bottom instead of a keel, which allowed the ship to move in as little as four feet of water. A sophisticated ballast system brought sea water into tanks on the ship, which

LST 325 on the Ohio River. *Ronald May*.

forced the ship down lower in the water for stabilization in crossing the open seas. As the ship approached land, the water was pumped out, raising the ship, so that it could get close to land. After the tide went out, the ship, with its flat bottom, could rest on dry ground.[520]

Once at its desired location, the ship's crew opened its massive bow doors and lowered the ramp. The tanks and other vehicles were then driven down the ramp and onto the beach.

The anchor was lowered while the ship was still in deep water, and a long cable attached to a winch at the ship's stern was extended, allowing the ship to continue its movement toward land. Once the ship was unloaded and ready to head back to sea, the winch rolled up the cable and pulled the ship backward until it was in water deep enough to raise the anchor and move under normal power.

The genius of the flatbottom design had its curse as well. Instead of cutting through the water, the flatbottom ship slapped the water as it moved across the ocean. It was a rough and dangerous ride for the crew. Having a top speed of only ten miles per hour (11.6 knots), it was unable to outrun an attack from enemy ships. Although equipped with guns on its deck, both 40mm and 20mm, they were used mostly for antiaircraft defense and were of little help when the ship came under attack from enemy vessels.[521]

Perhaps because the navy believed that so many of the ships would be lost in battle, it didn't even bother to give names to the LSTs, only numbers.[522] That it was considered a disposable ship did not take away anything from its importance, especially to the men who served on it. Native Hoosier Robert Patterson was one of those sailors.

Patterson was born on May 27, 1925, in Linnsburg, Indiana, a small town ten miles southeast of Crawfordsville. When he graduated from Waveland High School in 1943, the United States was in the middle of World War II. One year after graduating, Patterson enlisted in the navy.[523]

Bob Patterson. *Bob Patterson.*

Following his training, Patterson was assigned as a cook on LST 1078. The brand-new ship was commissioned on May 15, 1945. After its shakedown cruise in the Chesapeake Bay, it departed New York City in June 1945 and headed to Pearl Harbor via the Panama Canal. By the end of August, the ship had left Pearl Harbor on orders to take on army troops for occupation duty in Japan.[524]

Although the war in the Pacific had officially ended with Japan's surrender on September 2, the danger to the ship's crew persisted. There were still mines in the ocean that threatened ship movement. And this early after the surrender, no one knew for sure if Japan might decide to reengage in battle. Furthermore, there was the danger of crossing a foreboding ocean, especially on an LST. As Patterson explained, "The LST was flat-bottomed and terribly slow since it battered its way through the seas instead of slicing through the waves like a destroyer or cruiser. Little wonder that someone tagged it with the nickname 'Large Slow Target.'"[525]

After reaching Japan, Patterson rode the slap-happy ship to the Philippines and the islands of Guam, Saipan and Tinian before finally making it back to Pearl Harbor. He was honorably discharged in October 1946.[526]

LST 325 was just one of 1,051 similar ships made for the navy during World War II. The priority for making the ships was so high that the navy created new shipyard construction facilities along major waterways throughout the Midwest. Shipyards from Pennsylvania to Illinois worked feverishly to build the vessels essential for the Normandy landings. The Missouri Valley Bridge and Iron Company in Evansville, Indiana, built 171 LSTs, becoming the largest producer of the Cornfield Shipyards.[527]

LST 325 was built at the navy shipyard in Philadelphia and launched on October 27, 1942. It was commissioned for naval service on February 1, 1943. Ensign Clifford E. Mosier, a forty-two-year-old career enlisted

Evansville
Shipyard welders.
*Evansville Museum
of Art, History, and
Science.*

navy man from Nebraska, became the first commanding officer and held the mantle of leadership until June 1945, one month after Germany's surrender.[528]

Following its shakedown cruise to test the ship and its men, LST 325 sailed to Oran, Algeria, in March 1943. For three months, the crew practiced loading and beaching operations in preparation for the upcoming invasion of Sicily. LST 325 made multiple landings in Sicily and then proceeded to Salerno, Italy, for another amphibious landing.[529]

By Thanksgiving 1943, the ship had arrived in Plymouth, England, to prepare for the upcoming invasion of Normandy. On June 5, 1944, LST 325 left Falmouth, England, with elements of the army's 5th Special Engineer Brigade and, following a twenty-four-hour delay due to bad weather, headed for Omaha Beach in Normandy. As part of Task Force B, it carried backup forces for the initial waves of troops going ashore. On June 7, LST 325 set anchor and unloaded its troops and vehicles into smaller personnel craft for their final transport to the beach.[530]

During the next eleven months (June 1944–April 1945), LST 325 traversed the English Channel forty-three times and unloaded troops and vehicles at Omaha, Utah, Gold and Juno Beaches. In late December 1944, it engaged in rescue operations for more than seven hundred men of troop transport *Empire Javelin*, which had been damaged by torpedoes off the coast of France.[531]

LST 325 departed in convoy for the United States on May 12, 1945. Caught in a major storm, a massive wave struck its bow, causing a critical crack across the main deck. The ship's fitters welded plates across the hull, which saved the ship and allowed it to continue its journey homeward. It arrived in Norfolk, Virginia, on May 31, 1945, and then proceeded to the shipyard in New Orleans for repairs. It was on a shakedown cruise in August when Japan surrendered, bringing World War II to an end.

On July 2, 1946, LST 325 was officially decommissioned from naval service. It was reactivated three times, once during the Korean War and twice during the Vietnam War, before it was decommissioned by the U.S. Navy for the last time in 1963.[532]

In May 1964, the ship was purchased by Greece and transferred to the Greek navy. It was given a new name, *Syros* (L-144), and served for the next thirty-five years with the Greek navy. In 1999, it was deactivated for the fifth time in its life. It would have been mothballed if it had not been for a chance discovery of the ship by a veteran U.S. sailor who had once served on LSTs.[533]

Ed Strobel was visiting friends in Greece in 1995 when he learned of that government's decision to mothball the old LST ships that had been acquired from the United States. Strobel was a member of the LST Association back home in Decatur, Illinois. It consisted of ten thousand former crew members of LST ships who wanted to preserve the history of that ship's service. The organization was interested in locating an LST to turn it into a memorial ship and national museum. That effort, however, had proven difficult, as the United States had not kept any of the LSTs used in World War II or Korea. All of them had been either mothballed, sold or given away to other countries.[534]

Strobel inquired through friends and learned that the Greek government was willing to donate to the United States one of the old LSTs so that it could be turned into a museum. LST 325/*Syros* was the one selected of the seven former U.S. LST ships that Greece owned.[535]

The USS LST Ship Memorial Inc. acquired the ship in 2000 and prepared to bring it back to the United States with an all-volunteer crew, consisting of former navy sailors who had once served on LSTs during World War II and Korea. The men, most of whom were in their seventies at the time, paid their own way to Greece and pitched in for supplies. They also endured one-hundred-degree heat on board the ship during the voyage.[536]

LST 325 departed from the island of Crete in November 2000. Its return home to the United States was not without incident. After a short time at sea, the ship lost one of its engines and its steering wheel. The crew had to jerry-rig a new wheel to steer the hobbled ship. The aged relic somehow made it to Gibraltar, Spain, for the needed repairs.[537]

Crossing the Atlantic Ocean was also no picnic. Wind from the west brought heavy storms, which buffeted the fifty-eight-year-old ship. Nevertheless, the dedication of its captain, Robert Jornlin, and the all-volunteer veteran crew successfully sailed the ship across the 6,500 miles of open water and brought it to a temporary new home in Mobile, Alabama, on January 10, 2001.[538]

Two years later, after receiving some much-needed repairs and restoration, it once again moved on its own power and traveled up the Mississippi and Ohio Rivers, making several ports of call. In 2005, the ship traveled up the East Coast and stopped in several port cities before arriving at its new homeport in Evansville, Indiana. The city warmly welcomed the ship and adopted the ship as its own. Except for short cruises every fall, it has remained there ever since.[539]

Today, LST 325 is one of only two existing World War II LST ships in the United States. The other remaining ship, LST 393, is in Muskegon, Michigan, and serves as a museum.[540] Of the two, LST 325 is the only fully operational ship. It is used each June for a simulated amphibious invasion along the Ohio River during Evansville's Annual Shriners Freedom Fest. Every September, the ship travels up a river or across a coastline to allow

LST 325, open bow doors, with view of Ohio River. *Ronald May.*

more people to view it and learn of its proud heritage of service in combat. The ship has also appeared in several videos and movies. Its most important function, however, is as a museum for that class of ship and a memorial for the men who once served on them.

LST 325 is located at 6510 Northwest Riverside Drive, adjacent to downtown Evansville's waterfront along the popular river walkway. The ship is in port eleven months out of the year and is open for tours. Knowledgeable guides take visitors throughout the ship and show them its unique design and special equipment that allowed it to land vehicles and troops ashore. The visitors center at the docking facility traces the history of the ship with exhibits and information.

World War II history is afloat in Indiana, and it is well worth seeing the ship and walking its historic decks.[541]

To learn more about LST 325, visit the website at www.lstmemorial.org.

27

INDIANA ARMY
AMMUNITION PLANT

Charlestown, Indiana, was founded in 1808, eight years before Indiana became a state. Located along the Ohio River, thirteen miles northeast of Louisville, the town's early claim to fame was being the birthplace of Jonathan Jennings, the first governor of Indiana. A new claim to fame came during World War II.

In 1939, the town's population was 750 residents.[542] It was a small, quaint and quiet town set in a rural area. But all that ended abruptly in 1940. That was the same year that Congress approved the Munitions Program, part of the National Defense Appropriations Act, which opened the way for constructing new ammunition plants in the United States. Charlestown was selected to become the first single-base smokeless powder plant.[543] The production of smokeless powder was needed for the war effort because "traditional smoke obscured combatants' vision and revealed their location."[544]

Already by 1939, the federal government had selected Charlestown and parts of Clark County as the site for a new ammunition plant. Its decision was based on the town's inland location from the coast, undeveloped land, railroad access, adequate water and transportation via the Ohio River and its potential labor pool with the city's location near Jeffersonville, Indiana, and Louisville, Kentucky.[545]

Following the July 1940 announcement that Charlestown was selected as the plant site, the federal government began buying large chunks of land, while thirteen thousand construction workers from all over the country flooded the small town and began building the plant. "Street corner markets popped up, schools overflowed with new students, and rental prices for rooms became astronomically high. Rooms in town were rented per shift for sleeping purposes, and garages and chicken huts were converted into makeshift bedrooms. Seventeen mobile home parks were built that contained more units than Charlestown's 250 homes."[546] Some people put up tents for their quarters, and others chose to sleep in their cars. Chairs in barbershops were rented out for sleeping. Even the local jail became temporary quarters for some workers.[547]

The master plan involved building three different manufacturing facilities. On May 31, 1942, the Indiana Ordnance Works Plant No. 1 (IOW1) was the first facility to be completed. Even before its completion, it had begun producing smokeless and black powder as early as April 11.[548] By July of the same year, the plant had produced twice the powder the United States had made the previous year.[549] At its peak, the plant employed 9,442 workers, 25 percent of whom were women.[550]

Indiana Ordnance Works, September 26, 1941. *Charlestown Library.*

The second facility, the Hoosier Ordnance Plant (HOP), was completed in February 1942. It was designed for the loading, assembling and packaging of the powder from IOW1 which, after being weighed, was placed in bags that were sewn shut. The powder bags were used for cannons, artillery and mortars. The Bag Manufacturing Plant in HOP had 1,500 sewing machines used for stitching the bags filled with the powder. "The hallmark product was a 16-inch diameter bag of powder that when loaded six deep in the breach of a battleship's turret, could propel 2,750-pound bullet 25 miles."[551] HOP had a peak of 8,902 workers, two-thirds of whom were women.[552]

Construction on Indiana Ordnance Works 2 (IOW2), the rocket propellant plant, didn't begin until December 1944. The footprint for the plant spread across almost eight thousand acres to ensure safety in the handling of nitroglycerine. The plant operated for only a brief period before being shut down because of the war's end. During the six weeks of production from July to August 1945, the plant produced 292,700 pounds of rocket powder used for bazookas and rocket weapons.[553] The peak of contractors and officials reached 17,585 by June 1945.[554] For a short time, 1,000 German POWs helped in the construction of the camp and were housed there. They were returned to Germany a few months later when the war ended.[555]

While there were several name changes for the plants over the years, by 1963 all three plants had come under the combined name of the Indiana Army Ammunition Plant.[556]

Roughly 10 percent of the workers in the three plants were African American. Although they were initially given only unskilled positions, the demand for workers eventually opened opportunities for them to serve in skilled jobs. Housing and schooling, however, remained segregated and usually meant poorer living conditions.[557]

There were 1,700 buildings at IOW1, HOP and IOW2 that were built on a land mass of 19,200 acres. The project cost reached $133.4 million. The facilities included 34 administrative buildings, 2 hospitals, 3 research and design buildings, 114 standard magazines, 21 utility buildings, 176 igloo storage units, 149 warehouses and 566 miscellaneous buildings.[558] The massive property also consisted of 190 miles of roads, 92 miles of railroad track and more than 30 miles of fencing.[559]

One man who knew the fence line well was Myron Kelly. Kelly was born in 1915 in Ripley County, Indiana, and graduated from Dillsboro High School in 1933. He landed a job at the ammunition plant property in an unintended and most unlikely way: a speeding ticket. In the summer of 1940, Kelly was driving his car hard between Milan and Dillsboro—he was trying to blow out carburetor cleaner from the engine—when a state policeman stopped him and issued him a speeding ticket. Kelly shook the officer's hand and commended him for doing his job. One day later, the same officer came to Kelly's workplace and offered him a job supervising the clearing of land for the powder plant in Charlestown. Kelly accepted.[560]

From June 1 to August 18, 1941, Kelly and his crew used 22,429 sticks of dynamite and 11,165 dynamite caps to clear the land. Because sparks could ignite the dynamite, it was transported to each site by horses fitted with brass shoes. When the clearing was finished, Kelly was assigned to guard the property's thirteen-plus miles of fence

Myron Kelly. *Bob Kelly.*

line. He was on duty when the news came that the Japanese had attacked Pearl Harbor.[561]

On September 11, 1942, Kelly joined the U.S. Army Air Corps. He became a supervisor over a crew of eleven mechanics servicing bombers at Base Air Depot 1 Burtonwood, in Lancashire, England, near the city of Warrington. He returned home in the fall of 1945 and was honorably discharged on December 7, 1945, after three years and two months of military service.[562]

Considering the danger of possible explosions, all three plants put a priority on worker safety. "Buildings were spread far from one another to diminish the chance of a mass explosion, and copper-lined transfer chutes were utilized that reduced airborne powder movement. Emergency slides were installed in some buildings to provide a quick escape. Conductive shoes were issued for workers to reduce static electricity, and employees were searched daily for matches and other hazardous materials."[563] Those efforts made accidents rare, but they did occur. In the summer of 1944, a fire broke out in a blending tower and killed three people.[564]

By the spring of 1941, Charlestown's population had grown to more than three thousand, nearly a 400 percent increase from the 1939 population. In 1942, one projection estimated that fifty thousand people were employed as construction or production workers. When the facilities were completed, many of the construction workers transferred to jobs in the manufacturing facilities.[565]

The three plants' operations made a significant contribution to the war effort overseas, producing more than 1 billion pounds of the smokeless powder. That amount exceeded the total amount of explosives produced by the United States in World War I. It was more than enough to earn the coveted Army-Navy "E" Award.[566]

Following the end of the war, Charlestown reverted to its former size almost as quickly as it had expanded in 1940. Masses of workers left the town in search of other jobs as the plants were put in a standby mode. Temporary structures were removed, traffic disappeared and the tempo of life returned to its lazy, prewar pace.[567]

The plants were reactivated during the Korean and Vietnam Conflicts, and once again, the town experienced surges in population and activity. All operations of the plants were halted in 1991, and they were closed for good in 1992. The government sold the plants, some to private owners, and much of IOW2 became the Charlestown State Park in 1996. Today, part of the land from IOW1 is the River Ridge Commerce Center and is used for factories and warehouses. Some of the original administrative buildings from IOW1 remain and are used for office and retail space.[568]

Igloo-style Ground Ordnance Storage, Indiana Ordnance Works. *Ronald May.*

In 2007, the Indiana Historical Bureau officially recognized the contribution of the former Indiana Army Ammunition Plant with the placement of a historical marker along Corporate Drive, just outside the Charlestown limits. Behind the marker a short distance is one of the igloo-style ground-storage units from the original plant.[569] The igloo and the marker testify to an era long gone but mighty significant for the town that produced and the armed forces that received the smokeless powder necessary for war and ultimately for victory.

For more information on Charlestown and the former powder plant, visit the Charlestown Public Library, which has extensive archival material on both the town and the plant.

See also http://clarkco.lib.in.us/contentpages.asp?loc=118.

NOTES

Introduction

1. Wikipedia, "USS *Indiana* (BB-58)," accessed October 27, 2022, https://en.wikipedia.org/w/index.php?title=USS_Indiana_(BB-58)&oldid=1118019014.
2. Naval History and Heritage Command, "Indiana (BB 58)," accessed January 4, 2023, https://www.history.navy.mil/our-collections/photography/us-navy-ships/battleships/indiana-bb-58.html.
3. Ibid.
4. Benjamin M. Givens Jr., location of relics and artifacts of the USS *Indiana* BB-58, accessed October 27, 2022, https://www.oocities.org/pentagon/quarters/7858/relics.html; Wikipedia, "USS *Indiana* (BB-58)."
5. The gun mounts and mast had been on display in front of the stadium since 1966. They were donated by the U.S. Navy as a memorial to the men and women of Indiana who have served in the armed forces. The prow was added to the display in 2013 after being donated by a private collector in California. IU News Room, "USS Indiana Prow to Be Displayed at IU's Memorial Stadium, Honoring WWII Battleship," June 25, 2013, https://newsinfo.iu.edu/news-archive/24350.html.
6. Indiana War Memorial, "World War II Veterans Information Center," May 26, 2022, https://www.in.gov/iwm/veterans-memorial-plaza/world-war-ii-veterans-information-center/#:~:text=Under%20Construction.,those%20Hoosiers%20killed%20in%20action.

7. The Indiana War Memorial in Indianapolis has a room on the lower-level museum that showcases the contributions of many of the companies throughout Indiana that made products for the war effort. Divided into regions of the state, information boards identify the companies and what they produced during the war. There are also displays of some of those products. Visiting the exhibit space is one of the best ways to imagine the immensity of Indiana's manufacturing productivity during the war.

Part I

8. Sharon Porta, "Community War Memorial a Lasting Remembrance: Dedication Today for $3.2 million, Nine-Acre Memorial in Munster," *The Times* (Munster, IN), June 1, 2003, A9, https://www.newspapers.com/image/307830044/?terms=community%20war%20memorial.
9. Community Veterans Memorial, "World War II Pacific," accessed November 18, 2022, https://www.communityveteransmemorial.org/monuments/wwii-pacific.
10. Ibid., "World War II Europe," accessed November 18, 2022, https://www.communityveteransmemorial.org/monuments/wwii-europe.
11. Ibid.
12. Ibid., "WWII Home Front," accessed November 18, 2022, https://www.communityveteransmemorial.org/monuments/wwii-home.
13. During World War II, the steel mills of Northwest Indiana were some of the largest and most important factories that produced the precious metal so necessary for building tanks, jeeps, ships, weapons, mess kits and other products of war. That the production figures continued and even increased throughout World War II, when so many male workers were sent off to war, depended largely on the influx of women, who took jobs in the steel mills and became part of the legendary community of "Rosies." See Natasha Ishak, "From 'Magic City' to 'Murder Capital': 33 Haunting Photos of Gary, Indiana," All That's Interesting, December 18, 2019, https://allthatsinteresting.com/gary-indiana.
14. Ronald P. May, *Our Service Our Stories*, vol. 2 (Martinsville, IN: Fideli Publishing, 2018), 223–24.
15. Ibid., 225.

16. Ibid., 226, 228.
17. *The Times* (Munster, IN), "Flag Day Ceremonies Set for Munster Memorial," June 12, 2013, C6, https://www.newspapers.com/image/414444025/?terms=flag%20day%20ceremonies%20set%20for%20Munster%20Memorial&match=1.
18. Porta, "Community War Memorial," 1.
19. *The Times* (Munster, IN), "War Memorial to Gain New Name," August 30, 2007, 29, https://www.newspapers.com/image/310802636/?terms=war%20memorial%20to%20gain%20new%20name&match=1; Granite plaque at memorial.
20. Ibid.
21. Community Veterans Memorial, "Artists," accessed November 18, 2022, https://www.communityveteransmemorial.org/artists.
22. Wikipedia, "Omri Amrany," accessed November 17, 2022, https://en.wikipedia.org/w/index.php?title=Omri_Amrany&oldid=1087837833.
23. Sharon Porta, "Veterans Memorial Opens to Thousands," *The Times* (Munster, IN), June 2, 2003, A4, https://www.newspapers.com/image/307845451/?terms=%22Veterans%20memorial%20opens.
24. William P. Vogel, *Kingsbury, a Venture in Teamwork* (New York: Todd & Brown Inc., 1946), 9.
25. Ibid., 11.
26. Ibid., 20.
27. Ibid., 13. Kingsbury Ordnance Plant was fourth of seventy-three ordnance plants built around the country by the U.S. government before and during the years of World War II. Vogel, *Kingsbury*, 20.
28. Tom Ciecka, "Building 80 Miles of Road Inside Kingsbury Ordnance Plant," *Herald-Argus* (La Porte, IN), June 27, 1941.
29. Ibid.
30. Vogel, *Kingsbury*, 9.
31. United States of America Congressional Record: Proceedings and Debates of the 77th Congress, 1st Session, Appendix, Volume 87, Part 12, May 20, 1941, to July 14, 1941 (Washington, D.C.: U.S. Government Printing Office, 1941), page A2694, accessed October 6, 2022, Google Books, https://books.google.com.
32. Vogel, *Kingsbury*, 5.
33. Ibid., 11.
34. Ibid., 65.

35. *Indiana Magazine of History*, "The Kingsbury Ordnance Plant" (February 18, 2013), accessed October 6, 2022, https://indianapublicmedia.org/momentofindianahistory/kingsbury-ordnance-plant.

36. Ibid., 78.

37. Ibid., 66.

38. Ibid., 68.

39. Ronald P. May, *Our Service Our Stories*, vol. 3 (Martinsville, IN: Fideli Publishing, 2022), 221.

40. Ibid., 221–22.

41. Ibid., 222.

42. Ibid.

43. Ibid., 222–23.

44. Vogel, *Kingsbury*, 68.

45. May, *Our Service Our Stories*, 3:223.

46. *Indiana Magazine of History*, "Kingsbury Ordnance Plant." In 1944, the plant also hired 150 Black workers from Jamaica who had come to the United States to help harvest crops. Vogel, *Kingsbury*, 68.

47. May, *Our Service Our Stories*, 3:223.

48. Vogel, *Kingsbury*, 10.

49. Walter N. Smith, "Kingsbury Ordnance Plant Memo, Pertinent Dates," October 31, 1991, La Porte County Historical Society Museum Archives.

50. Wikipedia, "Kingsbury, Indiana," accessed October 6, 2022, https://en.wikipedia.org/w/index.php?title=Kingsbury,_Indiana&oldid=1111384207.

51. Veteran's National Memorial Shrine & Museum, "No Veteran Will Ever Be Forgotten," accessed November 21, 2022, https://honoringforever.org/node/70.

52. Robert Thomas, museum curator, during visit of author to the museum, November 11, 2022.

53. Ibid.

54. Ibid.

55. Thomas, curator.

56. Richard Lugar, U.S. Senate, Joe Brunson and Margaret Ray Ringenberg, Margaret Ray Ringenberg Collection, 1943, Personal Narrative, accessed November 21, 2022, https://www.loc.gov/item/afc2001001.54281.

57. Bud Mendenhall, during the author's visit to the museum, November 11, 2022.

58. Indiana Commission for Women, "Margaret Ray Ringenberg," June 26, 2022, https://www.in.gov/icw/search-results/?profile=icw&collection=agencies2&query=margaret%2Bray%2Bringenberg.

59. Thomas, curator; Family Search, "Harvey Richard Jessup," accessed November 22, 2022, https://ancestors.familysearch.org/en/LRN5-F75/harvey-richard-jessup-1921-2002.

60. Blood Chits of the China-Burma-India Theater of World War II, accessed November 19, 2022, https://cbi-theater.com/bloodchit/bloodchit.html.

61. Veteran's National Memorial Shrine & Museum, "About Us," accessed November 22, 2022, https://honoringforever.org/content/about-us.

62. Allen County War Memorial Coliseum, "About Us," 1, https://www.memorialcoliseum.com/about-us/history.

63. Otto H. Adams, *The Allen County War Memorial Coliseum*, a Project Gutenberg eBook, 1, accessed October 3, 2022, https://www.gutenberg.org/files/65372/65372-h/65372-h.htm.

64. Ibid., 4.

65. Adams, *Allen County War Memorial Coliseum*, 1.

66. Allen County War Memorial Coliseum, 5.

67. Adams, *Allen County War Memorial Coliseum*, 8.

68. Allen County War Memorial Coliseum, 29–30.

69. Adams, *Allen County War Memorial Coliseum*, 6.

70. Ibid., 8.

71. Ibid., 9.

72. Ibid.

73. Allen County War Memorial Coliseum, 52.

74. Adams, *Allen County War Memorial Coliseum*, 14.

75. Ibid., 14, 16.

76. Ibid., 9.

77. Jeffrey Alderton, "Lonaconing Native, Victim of Pearl Harbor Attack, Positively Identified through DNA," *Cumberland (MD) Times-News*, August 15, 2018, accessed October 4, 2022, https://www.times-news.com/news/local_news/lonaconing-native-victim-of-pearl-harbor-attack-positively-identified-through/article_c4de4d78-d43b-5415-8f7d-fa9e023f9293.html#utm_campaign=blox&utm_source=facebook&utm_medium=social.

78. Ibid.

79. Ibid.

80. Ibid.

81. Allen County War Memorial Coliseum, "About Us."

82. The American Legion, "Veterans Plaza at Allen County War Memorial Coliseum," accessed September 8, 2022, https://www.legion.org/memorials/253718/veterans-plaza-allen-county-war-memorial-coliseum.

83. DeVonte' Dixon, "Veterans Memorial Mile Unveiled at Memorial Coliseum," FOX 55 (Fort Wayne, IN), July 22, 2021, accessed September 8, 2022, https://www.wfft.com/news/local/veterans-memorial-mile-unveiled-at-memorial-coliseum/article_e8d737b6-74cd-55ab-8cdd-9b64b6f727ae.html.

84. Ibid.

85. Dorothy Riker, "Baer Field Army Air Base," in *The Hoosier Training Ground: A History of Army and Navy Training Centers, Camps, Forts, Depots, and Other Military Installations Within the State Boundaries During World War II*, ed. Dorothy Riker (Bloomington: Indiana War History Commission, 1952), 85.

86. Ibid.

87. Ibid., 85–86.

88. Ibid., 88.

89. Ibid., 96.

90. 122nd Fighter Wing, "Baer Field Heritage Air Park," accessed September 30, 2022, https://www.122fw.ang.af.mil/About-Us/History/122FW-Air-Park.

91. Riker, "Baer Field Army Air Base," 97.

92. 122nd Fighter Wing, "Baer Field Heritage Air Park."

93. CURTISS C-46 COMMANDO, "Baer Field," accessed September 30, 2022, http://curtisscommando.e-monsite.com/pages/airfields/usa/baer-field.html.

94. Robert E. Tangeman Collection (AFC/2001/001/26773), Veterans History Project, American Folklife Center, Library of Congress, accessed September 30, 2022, https://memory.loc.gov/diglib/vhp/bib/loc.natlib.afc2001001.26773.

95. Robert E. Tangeman, interview by Carol Van Deman, Veterans History Project, American Folklife Center, Library of Congress, accessed September 30, 2022, https://memory.loc.gov/diglib/vhp/story/loc.natlib.afc2001001.26773/sr0001001.stream.

96. Ibid.

97. Ibid.

98. Ibid.

99. Ibid.

100. CURTISS C-46 COMMANDO, "Baer Field."

101. Robert E. Kearns Collection (AFC/2001/001/39067), Veterans History Project, American Folklife Center, Library of Congress, 2006, https://memory.loc.gov/diglib/vhp/bib/loc.natlib.afc2001001.39067.

102. Ibid.

103. Ibid.

104. CURTISS C-46 COMMANDO, "Baer Field."

105. Ibid.

106. 122nd Fighter Wing, "Baer Field Heritage Air Park."

107. Ibid., "122nd Fighter Wing History," accessed October 8, 2022, https://www.122fw.ang.af.mil/About-Us/History.

108. Ibid., "Baer Field Heritage Air Park."

109. Historic American Buildings Survey, Midwest Regional Office, HABS No. IN-301-A, National Park Service, Omaha, Nebraska, 2, accessed June 6, 2022, https://www.loc.gov/item/in0452; Library of Congress, "Grissom Air Force Base, Building No. 143, Peru, Miami County, In.," accessed June 6, 2022, https://www.loc.gov/item/in0452.

110. Ibid.

111. Richard Simmons, "Bunker Hill Naval Air Station," in *The Hoosier Training Ground: A History of Army and Navy Training Centers, Camps, Forts, Depots, and Other Military Installations Within the State Boundaries During World War II*, ed. Dorothy Riker (Bloomington: Indiana War History Commission, 1952), 114.

112. Wikipedia, "Grissom Air Reserve Base," accessed September 29, 2022, https://en.wikipedia.org/w/index.php?title=Grissom_Air_Reserve_Base&oldid=1107334630.

113. Simmons, "Bunker Hill Naval Air Station," 115.

114. Wikipedia, "Grissom Air Reserve Base."

115. Ibid.

116. Simmons, "Bunker Hill Naval Air Station," 125.

117. Ibid., 126.

118. Ibid.

119. *Indianapolis (IN) Star*, "Fertile Indiana Farm Year Ago Hoosier Station Now Turns Out Fliers for Navy," June 27, 1943, https://www.newspapers.com/image/legacy/104911650/?terms=Fertile%20Indiana%20Farm%20Year%20Ago%20Hoosier%20Station%20Now%20Turns%20Out%20Fliers%20for%20Navy&match=1.

120. Pearl Harbor Aviation Museum, "Boeing N2s-3 Stearman (Trainer)," February 1, 2022, https://www.pearlharboraviationmuseum.org/aircraft/boeing-n2s-3-stearman.

121. Simmons, "Bunker Hill Naval Air Station," 131.

122. Maureen (Rene) Williams, daughter of Joseph Durnin Sr., interview by Ronald P. May, July 7, 2022.

123. Ibid.

124. Ibid.

125. *Indianapolis (IN) Star*, "Williams and Pesky at Hoosier Base," September 12, 1943, https://www.newspapers.com/image/legacy/104898226/?terms=Williams%20and%20Pesky%20at%20Hoosier%20Base&match=1.

126. Williams interview.

127. *Indianapolis (IN) Star*, "Aviation Cadet Ted Williams Wins Diploma, Big Sendoff at Bunker Hill," December 7, 1943, https://www.newspapers.com/image/legacy/104922187/?terms=Aviation%20Cadet%20Ted%20Williams&match=1.

128. Williams interview.

129. Simmons, "Bunker Hill Naval Air Station," 126–27.

130. Ibid., 129.

131. Ibid., 131.

132. Ibid., 133.

133. *Kokomo (IN) Tribune*, "Bunker Hill Air Station to Be Closed," September 4, 1945, https://www.newspapers.com/image/legacy/41788696/?terms=Bunker%20Hill%20Air%20Station%20to%20be%20Closed&match=1.

134. Historic American Buildings Survey, Midwest Regional Office, HABS No. IN-301-A, 2.

135. Grissom Air Reserve Base, "History of Grissom Air Reserve Base, Indiana," accessed September 29, 2022, https://www.grissom.afrc.af.mil/About-Us/Fact-Sheets/Display/Article/174559/history-of-grissom-air-reserve-base-indiana.

136. Lauren Slagter, "New Memorial at Darrough Chapel Park Recognizes Military Families," *Kokomo Tribune* (Kokomo, IN), September 9, 2015, https://www.kokomotribune.com/news/new-memorial-at-darrough-chapel-park-recognizes-military-families/article_04a660d4-5660-11e5-8934-57e94699076b.html?mode=print.

137. Ibid.

138. May, *Our Service Our Stories*, 3:51–62.

139. Slagter, "New Memorial at Darrough Chapel Park."

140. IU Kokomo Newsroom, "Jerry Paul Plans to Leave Lasting Memorial," February 5, 2019, https://newsroom.iuk.edu/2019/february/jerry-paul-plans-to-leave-lasting-memorial.html.

141. Ibid.

142. National WWII Museum | New Orleans, "Research Starters: Women in World War II," accessed September 12, 2022, https://www.nationalww2museum.org/students-teachers/student-resources/research-starters/research-starters-women-world-war-ii.

143. Kali Martin, "It's Your War, Too: Women in World War II," National WWII Museum | New Orleans, March 12, 2020, https://www.nationalww2museum.org/war/articles/its-your-war-too-women-world-war-ii#:~:text=World%20Warkk%20II%20wasn%27t,call%20and%20served%20their%20country.

144. May, *Our Service Our Stories*, 2:285–86.

145. Betty Robling, who later married and moved to Mooresville, Indiana, died on January 12, 2022, at the age of ninety-five.

146. Justine Fletcher, "Was Coca-Cola Consumed by Soldiers in World War II?: FAQ: Coca-Cola Canada," accessed October 7, 2022, https://www.coca-cola.ca/faqs/coca-cola-faqs-history/Was-coca-cola-consumed-by-soldiers-in-world-war-II; Tyler H. Jones, "Historical Society to Offer Refresher on Coke's WWII Impact," *Brunswick (GA) News*, April 19, 2017, https://thebrunswicknews.com/life/historical-society-to-offer-refresher-on-coke-s-wwii-impact/article_cbbfd3e8-4f2b-57dd-808c-1cbec9ce0861.html.

147. Museum of the Soldier, "History," accessed October 7, 2022, http://museumofthesoldier.info/history.html.

148. Ibid., "Local Heroes," accessed October 9, 2022, http://museumofthesoldier.info/heroes.html; *Muncie (IN) Evening Press*, "Portland Sailor Listed as Missing," November 17, 1943, 7, accessed October 9, 2022, https://www.newspapers.com/image/legacy/249515655/?terms=Herbert+Bubp&match=1.

149. *Battle Creek (MI) Enquirer*, "Husband of Local Woman Is Missing," 6, accessed October 9, 2022, https://www.newspapers.com/image/legacy/204317948/?terms=Herbert+Bubp&match=1.

150. Uboat, "Cisco (SS-290)," front page, accessed October 9, 2022, https://uboat.net/allies/warships/ship/3036.html.

151. Naval History and Heritage Command, "Cisco (SS 290)," accessed October 10, 2022, https://www.history.navy.mil/research/library/

online-reading-room/title-list-alphabetically/u/united-states-submarine-losses/cisco-ss-290.html; On Eternal Patrol, "The Loss of USS Cisco (SS-290)," accessed October 10, 2022, https://www.oneternalpatrol.com/uss-cisco-290-loss.html.

152. A total of 52 submarines and 3,506 sailors were lost in service during World War II. National Park Service, "Submarines in World War II," accessed October 10, 2022, https://www.nps.gov/articles/000/submarines-in-world-war-ii.htm#:~:text=The%20American%20success%20came%20at,the%20War%3A%20about%2020%25.

153. Jay County, Indiana, "Green Park Cemetery," September 23, 2014, http://ingenweb.org/injay/Cemeteries/GreenPark/4GreenParkBo.html.

154. U.S. Naval Academy Virtual Memorial Hall, "James W. Coe, CDR, USN," accessed October 10, 2022, https://usnamemorialhall.org/index.php/JAMES_W._COE,_CDR,_USN.

155. *Palladium-Item* (Richmond, IN), "Daughter Born to Mrs. James W. Coe," April 9, 1944, 5, accessed October 10, 2022, https://www.newspapers.com/image/legacy/254924154/?terms=Coe&match=1.

156. Museum of the Soldier, Milo "Bill" Ludy display, Portland, Indiana, viewed August 6, 2022.

157. Ibid., John Carder display.

158. Ibid., Don F. Garner display.

159. Ibid., 1943 white M16A2 Half-Track vehicle display.

Part II

160. Ray E. Boomhower, *The Soldier's Friend: A Life of Ernie Pyle* (Indianapolis: Indiana Historical Society Press, 2006), 9, 18.

161. Ibid., 19–20.

162. Ibid., 20–22.

163. Ibid., 25.

164. Ibid., 30.

165. Ibid., 31.

166. Ibid., 32, 34.

167. Ibid., 42.

168. Ibid., 51.

169. Ibid., 54–55.

170. Ibid., 56–57. During the bombing of London, Americans also received live radio broadcasts from Edward R. Murrow, whose programs were called *This Is London*.

171. Ibid., 59.

172. Ibid., 62–63.

173. Ibid., 64.

174. Ibid., 72–73.

175. Ibid., 82–84.

176. Ibid., 85, 88.

177. Ibid., 88, 90.

178. Ibid., 106–7. In 1983, a Purple Heart was posthumously awarded to Pyle for his death. The award, rarely given to civilians, testified to the high regard the military had for Pyle and his work.

179. Ibid., 110.

180. Ibid., 2.

181. Indiana University also named one of its halls Ernie Pyle Hall. Formerly, its School of Journalism also carried Pyle's name.

182. In 2018, Congress approved a resolution drafted by Indiana's senators to make August 3, the date of Pyle's birth, National Ernie Pyle Day. The Ernie Pyle Legacy Foundation also helps keep Pyle's memory alive. See http://www.erniepylefoundation.org. Additionally, this chapter is a revision of two articles the author wrote in 2017 for the *Martinsville (IN) Reporter-Times*. Ronald P. May, "Hoosier Native Ernie Pyle: Master of the Written Word," *Martinsville (IN) Reporter-Times*, November 24, 2017, 1 and 6; Ronald P. May, "Stories from the Front: Ernie Pyle Chronicled the Experiences of the Common American Soldier," *Martinsville (IN) Reporter-Times*, December 1, 2017, 1 and 6.

183. Wikipedia, "V-1 Flying Bomb," accessed October 26, 2022, https://en.wikipedia.org/w/index.php?title=V-1_flying_bomb&oldid=1115898345.

184. Ibid.

185. Ibid.

186. Ibid.

187. Ibid.

188. Ibid.

189. May, *Our Service Our Stories*, 2:105, 108, 112. LCI(L) 517 participated in amphibious landings at Normandy, southern France and Italy. Welsh, who also served on an LCI in the Pacific Theater for a time, survived the war and returned to Indiana. He married Norma Lewellyn, also of Greenfield, in 1946, and the couple raised two children. Welsh worked for Eli Lilly and Dow Chemical companies before starting J.W. Welsh Engineering Consultants with his wife. He died at the age of ninety-four in 2015.

190. John W. Welsh, "My World War II Story," unpublished war memoir, 2005, revised 2006, 2007, 12.

191. Wikipedia, "V-1 Flying Bomb."

192. Ibid.

193. Ibid.

194. Putnam County Convention and Visitors Bureau, "Buzz Bomb Memorial," accessed October 26, 2022, http://web.archive.org/web/20141024030639/http://www.coveredbridgecountry.com/attractions/wwii-buzzbomb.

195. Heroic Relics, "V-1," accessed October 26, 2022, http://heroicrelics.org/greencastle/v-1/index.html.

196. Capitol & Washington, "Indiana Politicians by Letter," August 12, 2019, https://www.capitolandwashington.com/politicians/pol/7361; *Indianapolis (IN) News*, "Sgt. William Hoadley Killed in Luxembourg," November 13, 1944, 11, https://www.newspapers.com/image/314326731/?terms=William%20Hoadley&match=1.

197. Only two V-1s are on display in the United States today. The other one is located at the Smithsonian Institute in Washington, D.C.

198. This chapter is a revision of an article the author wrote in 2018 for the *Martinsville (IN) Reporter-Times*. Ronald P. May, "The 'Weapon of Vengeance': Germany's V-1 Flying Buzz Bomb," *Martinsville (IN) Reporter-Times*, January 31, 2018, 1 and 6.

199. Avon, Indiana, "WWII Memorial Park," accessed October 13, 2022, https://www.avongov.org/Facilities/Facility/Details/WWII-Memorial-Park-12.

200. Ibid.

201. Kara Kavensky, "Brigadier General Chet Wright," Towne Post Network, March 11, 2021, https://townepost.com/indiana/avon/brigadier-general-chet-wright.

202. Clyde Chester Wright Collection (AFC/2001/001/54367), Veterans History Project, American Folklife Center, Library of Congress, 18:00–24:00, https://memory.loc.gov/diglib/vhp/story/loc.natlib.afc2001001.54367.

203. Ibid.

204. Ibid.

205. Kavensky, "Brigadier General Chet Wright."

206. Ibid.

207. Bill Wolfe, e-mail message to the author, October 13, 2022.

208. Harry S. Truman Library, "Address Broadcast to the Armed Forces," April 17, 1945, https://www.trumanlibrary.gov/library/public-papers/5/address-broadcast-armed-forces.

209. American Presidency Project, "Inaugural Address: Dwight D. Eisenhower," January 20, 1953, https://www.presidency.ucsb.edu/documents/inaugural-address-3.

210. Brigadier General Clyde C. (Chet) Wright died on February 12, 2020, at the age of 101. It is estimated that 167,000 World War II veterans are still alive as of October 2022. Indiana is home to 4,583 of them. Each day, 180 World War II veterans die. National World War II Museum, "World War II Veteran Statistics," https://www.nationalww2museum.org/war/wwii-veteran-statistics.

211. Digital Rain, LLC, "Avon, Indiana's World War II Memorial Dedication Ceremony," YouTube, September 22, 2013, 35:08 to 35:38, https://www.youtube.com/watch?v=hAKS8I6oGqw.

212. Wikipedia, "Indiana World War Memorial Plaza," accessed October 28, 2022, https://en.wikipedia.org/w/index.php?title=Indiana_World_War_Memorial_Plaza&oldid=1116895748.

213. State of Indiana, "Indiana War Memorial Museum," May 26, 2022, https://www.in.gov/iwm/indiana-war-memorial-museum.

214. Mike Alexander, "Rededication of Memorial Fought," *Indianapolis (IN) News*, March 17, 1966, 1, https://www.newspapers.com/image/312126056/?terms=Rededication%20of%20Indiana%20War%20Memorial&match=1.

215. Wikipedia, "Indiana World War Memorial Plaza."

216. State of Indiana, "Indiana War Memorial Museum—Interior," May 26, 2022, https://www.in.gov/iwm/indiana-war-memorial-museum/indiana-war-memorial-museum-interior.

217. Ibid., "Indiana War Memorial Museum."

218. Ibid.

219. Ibid.

220. Ibid.

221. Ibid.

222. The Golden Book contains the handwritten names of twenty-five thousand IU students who served in wars dating back to the War of 1812 through World War II. More recent IU war veterans are included in the university's digitized version of the Golden Book, found in Memorial Hall, Indiana Memorial Union.

223. The Golden Book, "Edgar Whitcomb," accessed October 28, 2022, https://goldenbook.iu.edu/veteran-stories/whitcomb-edgar.html.

224. Edgar Whitcomb, *Escape from Corregidor* (Bloomington, IN: Author House, 1958, 2012). Whitcomb also wrote a second book about his early military service, *On Celestial Wings* (Montgomery, AL: Air University Press, Maxwell Air Force Base, 1995).

225. The Edgar Whitcomb Monument in Hayden, Indiana, was dedicated in 2014. Consisting of a limestone wall with a raised outline of Indiana, a bronze sculpture of Whitcomb wearing a suit from the waist up (in his era as governor) is recessed into the state's outline. On either side of the main wall are two smaller limestone walls with bronze art pieces: one that memorializes his escape from Corregidor during World War II and one that pays tribute to his yearlong feat of sailing around the world in 1996 at the age of seventy-one. The monument is located on the lawn outside the Hayden Historical Museum, which occupies the renovated house where Whitcomb grew up.

226. This chapter is a revision of an article the author wrote in 2017 for the *Martinsville (IN) Reporter-Times*. Ronald P. May, "The Crown Jewel: Downtown Indianapolis Boasts Impressive Veterans' Memorial," *Martinsville (IN) Reporter-Times*, July 26, 2017, 1, 4, 6.

227. Indiana War Memorial, inscription of letter, Indianapolis, Indiana.

228. *Speedway Flyer*, "That the Nation Might Live," June 22, 1945, Hoosier State Chronicles: Indiana's Digital Historic Newspaper Program, 3, accessed October 31, 2022, https://newspapers.library.in.gov/?a=d&d=SPWF19450622.1.3&e=-------en-20--1--txt-txIN-------. This was an ad that identified the names of 82 former graduates of Arsenal Technical High School in Indianapolis who had died in service to their country by the end of 1944 and whose gold stars had been placed on the school's service flag. By that point, 281 gold stars were on the flag.

229. World War II Memorial Registry, "World War II Missing in Action or Buried at Sea," accessed October 31, 2022, https://www.wwiimemorial.com/Registry/plaque_tabletsmissing.aspx?honoreeID=743469.

230. Rob Schneider, "Tribute in Stone So Long Deserved," *Indianapolis (IN) Star*, May 20, 1998, 2, accessed October 31, 2022, https://www.newspapers.com/image/107245248/?terms=Memorial.

231. Marcella Fleming and Kevin O'Neal, "Memorial Work Continues," *Indianapolis (IN) Star*, March 7, 1998, 19, https://www.newspapers.com/image/106415324/?terms=Memorial%20Work%20Continues&match=1.

232. Sharon Porta, "Written in Stone," *The Times* (Munster, IN), April 20, 1998, 5, https://www.newspapers.com/image/311066954/?terms=James%20McGregor&match=1.

233. Ibid., 1.

234. Dennis Royalty, "Touching Local Story Goes National," *Indianapolis (IN) News*, May 27, 1998, 5, accessed October 31, 2022, https://www.newspapers.com/image/313432631/?terms=Tom%20Brokaw&match=1.

235. Indiana War Memorial, "World War II Memorial," May 26, 2022, https://www.in.gov/iwm/american-legion-mall/world-war-ii-memorial.

236. Indiana War Memorials Foundation, "World War II Memorial," accessed November 1, 2022, https://www.indianawarmemorials.org/explore/world-war-ii-memorial.

237. William B. Rudy, "An Autobiography of William B. Rudy from Childhood through World War II," unpublished memoir, 9–10.

238. *Indianapolis (IN) Times*, "Hoosier Heroes: Three Reported Dead and Four Wounded," October 3, 1944, 10, accessed November 1, 2022, https://newspapers.library.in.gov/?a=d&d=IPT19441003.1.10&e=-------en-20--1--txt-txIN-------; Rudy, "Autobiography," 17.

239. Rudy, "Autobiography," 20, 24.

240. Ibid., 31, 38–39.

241. Rudy returned to Indiana University and graduated in 1947 from the School of Business.

242. Indiana War Memorial, inscription of letter, Indianapolis, Indiana.

243. Ibid.

244. Porta, "Written in Stone," 1.

245. Indiana War Memorial, inscription of poem, Indianapolis, Indiana.

246. Rob Schneider, "Inspired by Courage," *Indianapolis (IN) Star*, May 28, 1999, 2, accessed November 3, 2022, https://www.newspapers.com/image/107323587/?terms=National%20Medal%20of%20Honor%20Memorial&match=1.

247. Will Higgins, "Memorial Will Honor Medal of Honor Recipients," *Indianapolis (IN) Star*, January 27, 1999, 17–18, accessed November 3, 2022, https://www.newspapers.com/image/107305742/?terms=National%20Medal%20of%20Honor%20Memorial&match=1.

248. Wikipedia, "Medal of Honor Memorial (Indianapolis)," accessed November 2, 2022, https://en.wikipedia.org/w/index.php?title=Medal_of_Honor_Memorial_(Indianapolis)&oldid=1110391322.

249. Higgins, "Memorial Will Honor," 18. Biddle died in 2010, leaving Sammy L. Davis, a Vietnam veteran, as the only living Medal of Honor recipient from Indiana.

250. Schneider, "Inspired by Courage," 2.

251. Congressional Medal of Honor Society, "Medal of Honor FAQs," accessed November 3, 2022, https://www.cmohs.org/medal/faqs; Indiana Military Veterans Hall of Fame, "Medal of Honor," July 16, 2019, https://imvhof.com/medal-of-honor.

252. Indiana Military Veterans Hall of Fame, "Medal of Honor." A total of ninety-nine men from Indiana have been recipients of the Medal of Honor since its inception.

253. Together We Served, "McGee, William Douglas, Jr., PVT," accessed November 3, 2022, https://army.togetherweserved.com/army/servlet/tws.webapp.WebApp?cmd=ShadowBoxProfile&type=Person&ID=5979.

254. Congressional Medal of Honor Society, "William D McGee: World War II: U.S. Army: Medal of Honor Recipient," accessed November 3, 2022, https://www.cmohs.org/recipients/william-d-mcgee.

255. *Indianapolis (IN) Star*, "Pvt. McGee, City Hero, Given Medal of Honor Posthumously," February 24, 1946, 6, https://www.newspapers.com/image/104934736/?terms=William%20D.%20McGee&match=1.

256. Ibid.; Wikipedia, "William D. McGee," accessed November 3, 2022, https://en.wikipedia.org/w/index.php?title=William_D._McGee&oldid=1063027095.

257. Congressional Medal of Honor Society, "William D McGee."

258. *Indianapolis (IN) Star*, "Pvt. McGee, City Hero."

259. Congressional Medal of Honor Society, "Medical Aid & Corpsman Medal of Honor Recipients of the Medal of Honor," accessed November 3, 2022, https://www.cmohs.org/recipients/lists/medics-corpsmen.

260. Together We Served, "McGee, William Douglas."

261. National Medal of Honor Day is celebrated each year on March 25. The date coincides with the March 25, 1863 date when the first Medals of Honor were bestowed on six Union army soldiers during the Civil War. National Medal of Honor Day became a federal observance in 1991 after President George H.W. Bush signed a public law passed by Congress. A National Medal of Honor Museum in Arlington, Texas, is scheduled to open in 2024. Plans are also underway to build a National Medal of Honor Monument in Washington, D.C. For more information on the Medal of Honor, visit the Congressional Medal of Honor Society

website at https://www.cmohs.org. Additionally, this chapter is a revision of an article the author wrote in 2021 for the *Martinsville (IN) Reporter-Times*. Ronald P. May, "The Highest Honor: Commemorating Medal of Honor Recipients and Remembering Local WWII Hero," *Martinsville (IN) Reporter-Times*, March 23, 2021, 1 and 3.

262. Doug Stanton, *In Harm's Way: The Sinking of the USS* Indianapolis *and the Extraordinary Story of Its Survivors* (New York: Henry Holt and Company, 2001), 30, 37.

263. Ibid., 36, 42, 65.

264. Ibid., 68.

265. Ibid., 102.

266. Ibid., 111, 130.

267. Ibid., 135, 137.

268. Ibid., 141–42.

269. Ibid., 143.

270. Ibid., 165, 249.

271. Ibid., 133–34.

272. Ibid., 215.

273. Ibid., 225–27, 232–33.

274. Ibid., 233–50. Within a week of being rescued, 4 men died, reducing the number of total survivors to 317. In addition to the living survivors, 91 dead crewmen who were still floating in the water were picked up by rescue ships for body identification prior to sea burial. Stanton, *In Harm's Way*, 253–54.

275. Ibid., 254, 261.

276. Today, only 1 crewman remains of the 317 men who survived the tragedy.

277. Patrick J. Finneran, *U.S.S.* Indianapolis *Memorial Dedication* (Indianapolis, IN: USS *Indianapolis* (CA-35) Survivors Memorial Organization, 1995), 41.

278. The newly formed survivors group decided to meet every five years for future reunions, a frequency that continued until 1990, when the survivors decided to meet every two years. See Welton W. Harris II, "Memorial Caps Tribute for WWII Ship Survivors." *Indianapolis (IN) Star*, July 28, 1995, B1, https://search.proquest.com/newspapers/memorial-caps-tribute-wwii-ship-survivors/docview/240147215/se-2?accountid=57494.

279. Finneran, *U.S.S.* Indianapolis *Memorial Dedication*, 41.

280. Ibid., 42.

281. Ibid.

282. Marylou Murphy, *Only 317 Survived!: USS* Indianapolis *(CA-35): Navy's Worst Tragedy at Sea—880 Men Died* (Broomfield, CO: USS *Indianapolis* Survivors Organization, 2002), 378.

283. *The USS* Indianapolis *CA-35 National Memorial*, brochure in the collection of the Indiana State Museum, accessed February 12, 2021.

284. The story text for the memorial was written by Patrick Finneran.

285. Finneran, *U.S.S.* Indianapolis *Memorial Dedication*, 43–44.

286. *USS* Indianapolis *CA-35 National Memorial*, brochure.

287. Howard Smulevitz, "Indianapolis Memorial Nears Funding Goal; Ship's Model Unveiled," *Indianapolis (IN) Star*, January 11, 1994, https://search.proquest.com/newspapers/indianapolis-memorial-nears-funding-goal-ships/docview/240064591/se-2?accountid=57494.

288. Ibid.

289. William A. Davis, "Torpedoed Lives: Survivors of the Indianapolis Recall Navy's Worst Tragedy—and 50 Years of Nightmares," *Boston Globe*, July 27, 1995, 56, https://www.newspapers.com/image/440911540/?terms=The%20Boston%20Globe%20%28Boston%20MA%29.

290. Mary Lou Murphy, ed., *Lost at Sea but Not Forgotten* (Indianapolis, IN: Printing Partners, 2008), 5. Barksdale was one of twenty-nine Hoosiers aboard the *Indianapolis* who died. Ten others from Indiana survived the sinking.

291. Christina Nunez, "Paul Allen Discovers World War II Cruiser U.S.S. *Indianapolis* in Philippine Sea," *National Geographic*, May 3, 2021, https://www.nationalgeographic.com/history/article/uss-indianapolis-wreck-found; Stanton, *In Harm's Way*, 141.

292. Sam LaGrone, "USS Indianapolis Crew Awarded Congressional Gold Medal on 75th Anniversary of Sinking," *USNI News*, July 29, 2020, https://news.usni.org/2020/07/29/uss-indianapolis-crew-awarded-congressional-gold-medal-on-75th-anniversary-of-sinking.

293. Joseph S. Pete, "'Once-in-a-Lifetime Event' in Port of Ind.," *The Times* (Munster, IN), July 18, 2019, A10, https://www.newspapers.com/image/585253430/?terms=USS%20Indianapolis%20%28LCS%2017%29&match=1.

294. This chapter is a revision of two articles the author wrote in 2020 for the *Martinsville (IN) Reporter-Times* and a course paper for his master's degree: Ronald P. May, "Fateful Voyage for a Legendary Ship: USS *Indianapolis* Was Sunk 75 Years Ago After Delivering Top Secret Cargo," *Martinsville (IN) Reporter-Times*, July 31, 2022, 1, 6; Ronald P. May, "Remembering the USS *Indianapolis*: The Legacy Continues 75 Years

Later," *Martinsville (IN) Reporter-Times*, August 5, 2020, 1, 6; Ronald P. May, "The USS *Indianapolis* Memorial: An Examination of Its History, Purpose, and Meaning," Arizona State University, 2021, 2–10.

295. CANDLES Museum and Holocaust Education Center, "Eva Mozes Kor," accessed November 23, 2022, https://candlesholocaustmuseum. org/our-survivors/eva-kor/her-story/her-story.html.

296. Ibid., "Eva and Her Family's Last Days before the War," accessed November 23, 2022, https://candlesholocaustmuseum.org/our-survivors/eva-kor/her-story/her-story.html/title/read-about-eva-and-her-family-s-last-days-before-the-war.

297. Ibid.

298. Ibid.

299. Wikipedia, "Josef Mengele," accessed November 24, 2022, https://en.wikipedia.org/w/index.php?title=Josef_Mengele&oldid=1123203851.

300. CANDLES Museum and Holocaust Education Center, "Eva and Her Family's Last Days."

301. Wikipedia, "Eva Mozes Kor," accessed November 24, 2022, https://en.wikipedia.org/w/index.php?title=Eva_Mozes_Kor&oldid=1122294239.

302. Ibid.

303. Ibid.

304. CANDLES Museum and Holocaust Education Center, "Eva and Miriam After the War," accessed November 24, 2022, https://candlesholocaustmuseum.org/our-survivors/eva-kor/her-story/title/read-about-eva-and-miriam-after-the-war.

305. Eva Mozes Kor and Lisa Rojany Buccieri, *Surviving the Angel of Death: The True Story of a Mengele Twin in Auschwitz* (Terre Haute, IN: Tanglewood Publishing, 2009), 130.

306. Wikipedia, "Eva Mozes Kor."

307. CANDLES Museum and Holocaust Education Center, photo caption in museum exhibit.

308. Kor and Buccieri, *Surviving the Angel of Death*, 130.

309. Ibid., 131.

310. CANDLES Museum and Holocaust Education Center, "CANDLES Mission," accessed November 24, 2022, https://candlesholocaustmuseum.org/candles.

311. Kor and Buccieri, *Surviving the Angel of Death*, 132–33.

312. Wikipedia, "Josef Mengele."

313. CANDLES Museum and Holocaust Education Center, "Indiana's Only Holocaust Museum," accessed November 24, 2022, https://candlesholocaustmuseum.org/welcome.html.

314. Ibid., "Eva's Road to Forgiveness," accessed November 24, 2022, https://candlesholocaustmuseum.org/our-survivors/eva-kor/her-story/title/read-about-eva-s-road-to-forgiveness.

315. Kor and Buccieri, *Surviving the Angel of Death*, 133.

316 Wikipedia, "Eva Mozes Kor."

317. Eva Mozes Kor wrote three books about her life: *Surviving the Angel of Death, Echoes from Auschwitz* and *The Power of Forgiveness*, as well as a children's book, *Little Eva & Miriam in First Grade*.

318. CANDLES Museum and Holocaust Education Center, "Dimensions in Testimony Interactive Theater," accessed November 24, 2022, https://candlesholocaustmuseum.org/visit/exhibits.

319. Ibid., "Take a Trip with Candles," accessed November 24, 2022, https://candlesholocaustmuseum.org/trips.

320. This chapter is a revision of an article the author wrote in 2017 for the *Martinsville (IN) Reporter-Times*. Ronald P. May, "Jewish Twins and the Murders at Auschwitz: CANDLES Museum Tells the Story of Twin Survivors," *Martinsville (IN) Reporter-Times*, October 30, 2017, 1 and 6.

321. Yael Ksander, "A Soldier's Things: Veterans Memorial Museum of Terre Haute," Arts & Culture—Indiana Public Media, June 26, 2012, https://indianapublicmedia.org/arts/soldiers-veterans-memorial-museum-terre-haute.php.

322. Ibid.

323. Sue Loughlin, "Vets Museum Celebrates 5-Year Anniversary," *Tribune-Star* (Terre Haute, IN), November 11, 2017, https://www.tribstar.com/news/local_news/vets-museum-celebrates--year-anniversary/article_bad45fc1-5439-5940-86ef-7804180a71e3.html.

324. Ksander, "Soldier's Things."

325. Sue Loughlin, "Grand Opening of Veterans Memorial Museum of Terre Haute at Noon on Veterans Day," *Tribune-Star* (Terre Haute, IN), November 9, 2012, https://www.tribstar.com/news/local_news/grand-opening-of-veterans-memorial-museum-of-terre-haute-at/article_1492762a-446f-5489-9cea-ef70db530cee.html.

326. Loughlin, "Vets Museum Celebrates 5-Year Anniversary."

327. Howard Greninger, "A Day of Infamy, 75 Years After," *Tribune-Star* (Terre Haute, IN), December 7, 2016, https://www.tribstar.com/news/

local_news/a-day-of-infamy-75-years-after/article_c6b2c1cc-21bd-5e1e-96e1-1c8f142bc3c3.html.

328. Sue Loughlin, "Gerstmeyer High School WWII Honor Roll Again Viewable by the Public," *Tribune-Star* (Terre Haute, IN), November 11, 2016, https://www.tribstar.com/news/local_news/gerstmeyer-high-school-wwii-honor-roll-again-viewable-by-the-public/article_12038761-baa4-5bf9-b49f-8bbec219f635.html.

329. Alex Modesitt, "Seabee Recalls Post-War Duty on Japanese Isles," *Tribune-Star* (Terre Haute, IN), November 11, 2017, https://www.tribstar.com/news/local_news/seabee-recalls-post-war-duty-on-japanese-isles/article_164a2e10-292f-5944-a7e0-d2b33b9adeb9.html.

330. *Terre Haute (IN) Star*, "Pilot Missing on Anniversary of Day He Received His Wings," June 13, 1944.

331. *Indianapolis (IN) News*, "One of 6 Clay County Prisoners Liberated in Germany Is Home," May 7, 1945, 9, https://www.newspapers.com/image/314177821/?terms=Roger%20Withers&match=1.

332. "Kriegie" is how Allied prisoners of war often referred to themselves. It is a shortened slang form of the German word *kriegsgefangenen*, which means prisoner of war. Wiktionary, "Kriegie," accessed November 29, 2022, https://en.wiktionary.org/w/index.php?title=Kriegie&oldid=69814515.

333. *Indianapolis (IN) News*, "One of 6 Clay County Prisoners."

334. Loughlin, "Grand Opening of Veterans Memorial Museum."

335. Howard Greninger, "'Can You Imagine?' Wall of Honor Remembers Veterans Killed in Action," *Tribune Star* (Terre Haute, IN), November 11, 2022, https://www.tribstar.com/news/local_news/can-you-imagine-wall-of-honor-remembers-veterans-killed-in-action/article_a1b05a90-5ba0-11ed-a6be-a7fc73af6c43.html.

336. Ksander, "Soldier's Things."

337. Mary E. Arbuckle, "Camp Atterbury," in *The Hoosier Training Ground: A History of Army and Navy Training Centers, Camps, Forts, Depots, and Other Military Installations Within the State Boundaries During World War II*, ed. Dorothy Riker (Bloomington: Indiana War History Commission, 1952), 7.

338. Ibid., 11–12.

339. Atterbury-Muscatatuck, "Atterbury-Muscatatuck History," accessed November 29, 2022, https://www.atterburymuscatatuck.in.ng.mil/About/History.

340. Arbuckle, "Camp Atterbury," 23.

341. Wikipedia, "Camp Atterbury-Muscatatuck," accessed December 26, 2022, https://en.wikipedia.org/w/index.php?title=Camp_Atterbury-Muscatatuck&oldid=1125356934.

342. Arbuckle, "Camp Atterbury," 23.

343. Colonel Clifford M. Brown et al., "The History of Camp Atterbury," Indiana Military, accessed November 29, 2022, http://www.indianamilitary.org/Camp%20Atterbury/History/history_of_camp_atterbury.htm.

344. Ibid.

345. Arbuckle, "Camp Atterbury," 30–32.

346. Ibid.

347. Ibid., 42–44.

348. Ibid., 44–45.

349. Chester R. Burns, "Blocker, Truman Graves, Jr. (1909–1984)," Texas State Historical Association, accessed November 29, 2022, https://www.tshaonline.org/handbook/entries/blocker-truman-graves-jr.

350. Heather Green Wooten, "Drs. Truman and Virginia Blocker: Tales of a Texas Power Couple Presidential Address, East Texas Historical Association," *East Texas Historical Journal* 57, no. 1 (2019): 85–86, https://scholarworks.sfasu.edu/ethj/vol57/iss1/6.

351. Arbuckle, "Camp Atterbury," 49.

352. Wikipedia, "Camp Atterbury," accessed November 30, 2022, https://en.wikipedia.org/w/index.php?title=Camp_Atterbury&oldid=1124410934.

353. The prisoner of war camp and chapel portion of this chapter is a revision of an article the author wrote in 2018 for the *Martinsville (IN) Reporter-Times*. Ronald P. May, "A Place of Worship, a Touch of Home: Italian POWs Built a Chapel at Camp Atterbury," *Martinsville (IN) Reporter-Times*, February 24, 2018, 1, 6.

354. Mary Giorgio, "Pow 'Paradise': Camp Atterbury in South-Central Indiana," OrangeBean Indiana, December 1, 2019, https://orangebeanindiana.com/2019/11/13/pow-paradise-camp-atterbury-in-south-central-indiana. "Between 1941 and 1946, the United States detained over 500,000 German, Italian, and Japanese prisoners-of-war (POWs)." Of that number, fifteen thousand were interned at Camp Atterbury. Arbuckle, "Camp Atterbury," 41.

355. Giorgio, "Pow 'Paradise.'"

356. Elizabeth Gorenc, "POW Legacy Lives in Stone," U.S. Army, accessed December 31, 2022, https://www.army.mil/article/11945/pow_legacy_lives_in_stone.

357. *Camp Atterbury History*, booklet, prepared by the Atterbury-Bakalar Museum, Columbus, Indiana, 10.

358. Giorgio, "Pow 'Paradise.'"

359. Italian Heritage Society of Indiana, "Italian P.O.W. Chapel of Our Lady in the Meadow," September 7, 2022, https://italianheritage.org/about/italian-p-o-w-chapel-lady-meadow; "Camp Atterbury's POW Chapel Video," November 15, 2020, https://italianheritage.org/camp-atterburys-pow-chapel-video.

360. Rex Redifer, "The Life and Death of an Army Camp," *Indianapolis (IN) Star*, April 27, 1980, section 5, 1–2, https://www.newspapers.com/image/107597043.

361. Arbuckle, "Camp Atterbury," 39–41.

362. Italian Heritage Society of Indiana, "Camp Atterbury's POW Chapel Video."

363. Ryan Trares, "Chapel in the Meadow: Learn about Italian POWs at Camp Atterbury," *Daily Journal* (Franklin, IN), February 16, 2017, https://dailyjournal.net/2017/02/16/chapel_in_the_meadow_.

364. Wikipedia, "Camp Atterbury-Muscatatuck."

365. National Archives, "Executive Order 9066: Resulting in Japanese-American Incarceration (1942)," accessed September 24, 2022, https://www.archives.gov/milestone-documents/executive-order-9066.

366. May, *Our Service Our Stories*, 3:274–75.

367. Ibid., 274.

368. Ibid., 276.

369. Brian Niiya, "Minidoka," Densho Encyclopedia, accessed September 14, 2021, https://encyclopedia.densho.org/Minidoka.

370. May, *Our Service Our Stories*, 3:282.

371. Ibid., 285.

372. Richard Reeves, *Infamy: The Shocking Story of the Japanese American Internment in World War II* (New York: Picador, 2015), 196–97.

373. Eric Langowski, "Education Denied: Indiana University's Japanese American Ban, 1942 to 1945," *Indiana Magazine of History* 115, no. 2 (2019): 65, accessed September 26, 2022, muse.jhu.edu/article/813872.

374. May, *Our Service Our Stories*, 3:288.

375. "Only 630 students—about one-fifth of the total 3,252 Nisei enrolled at West Coast institutions in 1941—were able to gain the sponsorship of a handful of college administrators and thus avoid the concentration camps altogether.…Approximately three-quarters of American

institutions would deny admissions to Nisei students during the war."
Langowski, "Education Denied," 74, 75.

376. Ibid., 67.

377. Ibid., 102; Salome Cloteaux, "IU Dedicates Japanese American Ban Memorial in Ceremony Friday," *Indiana Daily Student* (Bloomington, IN), November 12, 2021, accessed September 26, 2022, https://www.idsnews.com/article/2021/11/iu-dedicates-japanese-american-ban-memorial-in-ceremony-friday#.

378. Eric Langowski, "Indiana University Apologizes for Japanese American Ban," *Pacific Citizen* (Los Angeles, CA), August 28, 2020, accessed September 18, 2022, https://www.pacificcitizen.org/indiana-university-apologizes-for-japanese-american-ban.

379. Ibid.

380. Cloteaux, "IU Dedicates Japanese American Ban Memorial."

381. Thanks to alumni Eric Langowski's efforts and others within the university and beyond, IU is one of the first large universities outside the West Coast to officially acknowledge and seek to redress the issue of denying Japanese students' admission during the war. Langowski, "Education Denied," 112.

382. Ibid., 103.

383. May, *Our Service Our Stories*, 3:291–92.

384. Dorothy Riker, "Atterbury Army Air Base," in *The Hoosier Training Ground: A History of Army and Navy Training Centers, Camps, Forts, Depots, and Other Military Installations Within the State Boundaries During World War II*, ed. Dorothy Riker (Bloomington: Indiana War History Commission, 1952), 80, 82.

385. Ibid., 82.

386. Ibid., 83.

387. The British had their own version of a glider, the Horsa. It was larger than the WACO and was also used extensively during aerial operations in Europe.

388. Leon B. Spencer Jr., "WACO CG-4A Glider," Atterbury-Bakalar Air Museum, Columbus, Indiana, 2019, 1.

389. "In training missions, the gliders were reused many times. However, after a combat mission, only about 5% of the gliders could be repaired and reused." Spencer, "WACO CG-4A Glider," 1.

390. Leon Spencer, "Eight Missions—Serials," National WWII Glider Pilots Committee, Silent Wings Museum Foundation, accessed October 20, 2022, https://www.ww2gp.org/war/missions.

391. Find A Grave, "William Bruce Dalton (1914–2007)," accessed October 14, 2022, https://www.findagrave.com/memorial/38583429/william-bruce-dalton.

392. William Bruce Dalton Collection (AFC/2001/001/25571), Veterans History Project, American Folklife Center, Library of Congress, 2004, https://memory.loc.gov/diglib/vhp/bib/loc.natlib.afc2001001.25571.

393. Ibid.

394. Find A Grave, "William Bruce Dalton."

395. Atterbury-Bakalar Air Museum, "The Airport at Columbus, Indiana," Columbus, Indiana, 2021, 5–6.

396. Ibid., "History of Bakalar Air Force Base."

397. Ibid., "Grand Re-Opening," accessed October 20, 2022, https://www.atterburybakalarairmuseum.org/grand-re-opening.html.

398. Henry McCawley, "Ice Cream, Clothes Came Second to City Involvement," *The Republic* (Columbus, IN), May 15, 2007, 9, https://www.newspapers.com/image/legacy/148946786/?terms=Bruce+Dalton&match=1.

399. Atterbury-Bakalar Air Museum, "William 'Bruce' Dalton Media Center," accessed October 14, 2022, https://www.atterburybakalarairmuseum.org/media-center.html.

400. Ibid., "The Jeanne Lewellen Norbeck Memorial Chapel," accessed October 14, 2022, https://www.atterburybakalarairmuseum.org/memorial-chapel.html.

401. Rod Lewellen, "Jeanne Lewellen Norbeck: WASP Pilot—World War 2," Atterbury-Bakalar Air Museum, Columbus, Indiana, 2017, 1–2.

402. Ibid., 3–4.

403. Ibid., 4.

404. Ibid., 6.

405. Ibid., 8.

Part III

406. Indiana Military Museum, "History of the Museum: Jim Osborne's Story-Video," accessed December 9, 2022, https://www.indianamilitarymuseum.com/museum-history.

407. Ibid.

408. Ibid.

409. Ibid., "History of the Museum: History of the IMM—Video," accessed December 9, 2022, https://www.indianamilitarymuseum.com/museum-history.

410. Ibid.

411. Ibid.

412. Wikipedia, "Red Skelton," accessed December 10, 2022, https://en.wikipedia.org/w/index.php?title=Red_Skelton&oldid=1126329452.

413. Red Skelton Museum of American Comedy at Vincennes, "I Dood It," museum panels.

414. Wikipedia, "Red Skelton."

415. This chapter is a revision of an article the author wrote in 2018 for the *Martinsville (IN) Reporter-Times*. Ronald P. May, "The Indiana Military Museum: Another Jewel for Historic Vincennes," *Martinsville (IN) Reporter-Times*, March 24, 2018, 1 and 6.

416. Dorothy Riker, "Crane Naval Ammunition Depot," in *The Hoosier Training Ground: A History of Army and Navy Training Centers, Camps, Forts, Depots, and Other Military Installations Within the State Boundaries During World War II*, ed. Dorothy Riker (Bloomington: Indiana War History Commission, 1952), 262–63.

417. Ibid., 264.

418. An ammunition depot had been built in Hawthorn, Nevada, in 1928 to serve the Pacific fleet. Two more ammunition depots for the navy were added in the central United States shortly after the one built in Indiana. One was in Hastings, Nebraska, and the other in Macalester, Oklahoma. Margaret "Peggy" Julian and Anthony "Tony" Haag, *The World War II History of NAD Crane* (N.p.: Blurb, 2012, 2015), iii.

419. Riker, "Crane Naval Ammunition Depot," 264–65; Julian and Haag, *World War II History of NAD Crane*, ii–iii.

420. Riker, "Crane Naval Ammunition Depot," 265–66.

421. Julian and Haag, *World War II History of NAD Crane*, 1–2.

422. Riker, "Crane Naval Ammunition Depot," 276–77; Wikipedia, "William M. Crane," accessed December 1, 2022, https://en.wikipedia.org/w/index.php?title=William_M._Crane&oldid=1115583721.

423. Julian and Haag, *World War II History of NAD Crane*, i.

424. Robert L. Reid and Thomas E. Rodgers, *A Good Neighbor: The First Fifty Years of Crane* (Evansville: Historic Indiana Project, University of Southern Indiana, 1991), 53.

425. Naval History and Heritage Command, "Building the Navy's Bases in World War II (Volume I, Part II)," 340, accessed December 1, 2022,

https://www.history.navy.mil/content/history/nhhc/research/library/online-reading-room/title-list-alphabetically/b/building-the-navys-bases/building-the-navys-bases-vol-1-part-II.html.

426. Riker, "Crane Naval Ammunition Depot," 270–71.

427. Julian and Haag, *World War II History of NAD Crane*, 13.

428. Reid and Rodgers, *Good Neighbor*, 53.

429. Julian and Haag, *World War II History of NAD Crane*, 8.

430. Raymond Thomas, interview by Thomas Rogers, May 21, 1991, Oral History Collection, David L. Rice Library, University of Southern Indiana, University Archives and Special Collections, accessed December 1, 2022, https://digitalarchives.usi.edu/digital/collection/p17218coll1/id/11190/rec/2.

431. Ibid.

432. Reid and Rodgers, *Good Neighbor*, 71.

433. Ibid., 73.

434. Julian and Haag, *World War II History of NAD Crane*, 8.

435. Riker, "Crane Naval Ammunition Depot," 278.

436. Reid and Rodgers, *Good Neighbor*, 51.

437. Riker, "Crane Naval Ammunition Depot," 284.

438. Reid and Rodgers, *Good Neighbor*, 71.

439. Julian and Haag, *World War II History of NAD Crane*, 13.

440. Naval Sea Systems Command, "NSWC Crane Division," accessed December 1, 2022, https://www.navsea.navy.mil/Home/Warfare-Centers/NSWC-Crane/Who-We-Are/#:~:text=NSWC%20Crane%20is%20one%20of,are%20scientists%2C%20engineers%20and%20technicians.

441. Dorothy Riker, "The Freeman Army Air Base," in *The Hoosier Training Ground: A History of Army and Navy Training Centers, Camps, Forts, Depots, and Other Military Installations Within the State Boundaries During World War II*, ed. Dorothy Riker (Bloomington: Indiana War History Commission, 1952), 139.

442. Larry Bothe, "A Brief History of Freeman Field—the Fact Sheet," Freeman Army Airfield Museum, June 2021, https://freemanarmyairfieldmuseum.org/history-of-the-airfield; Riker, "Freeman Army Air Base," 141.

443. Bothe, "Brief History of Freeman Field—the Fact Sheet."

444. Museum volunteer, Freeman Army Airfield Museum, during a tour taken by the author on July 27, 2018.

445. Wikipedia, "Link Trainer," accessed December 2, 2022, https://en.wikipedia.org/w/index.php?title=Link_Trainer&oldid=1120241589;

"Learning to Fly Blind," Link Trainer Promotional Poster, Freeman Army Airfield Museum.

446. Bothe, "Brief History of Freeman Field—the Fact Sheet"; Riker, "Crane Naval Ammunition Depot," 144.

447. Freeman Army Airfield Museum, "Lt. Ken McKain, Seymour Native, WW-II Hero," information sheet.

448. *The Tribune* (Seymour, IN), "Miss Alma Mann to Be Bride of Aviation Cadet Kenneth McKain," September 3, 1943, 3, https://www.newspapers.com/image/161978445/?terms=Kenneth%20McKain&match=1.

449. Freeman Army Airfield Museum, "Lt. Ken McKain."

450. Bothe, "Brief History of Freeman Field—the Fact Sheet"; Riker, "Crane Naval Ammunition Depot," 152.

451. Freeman Army Airfield introductory video, Freeman Army Airfield Museum, July 27, 2018.

452. Larry Bothe, "Freeman Field Mutiny," Freeman Army Airfield Museum, August 23, 2020, https://freemanarmyairfieldmuseum.org/tuskegee-airmen.

453. "Army Regulation 210-10, published in 1940, required that any officers club on a post must be open to any officer on the post." East Coast Chapter Tuskegee Airmen Inc., "The Tuskegee Airmen Story: The 477th Bombardment Group (M) (Colored)," accessed December 6, 2022, https://ecctai.org/tuskegee-477th-bombardment-group.

454. Connie Nappier Jr. Collection (AFC/2001/001/67520), Veterans History Project, American Folklife Center, Library of Congress, https://www.loc.gov/item/afc2001001.67520.

455. Ibid.

456. Ibid.

457. Bothe, "Freeman Field Mutiny."

458. Bothe, "Brief History of Freeman Field—the Fact Sheet."

459. Museum volunteer, Freeman Army Airfield Museum.

460. Freeman Army Airfield introductory video.

461. Bothe, "Brief History of Freeman Field—the Fact Sheet."

462. Logan Nye, "These Were the Helicopters of World War II," We Are the Mighty, November 22, 2022, https://www.wearethemighty.com/popular/military-helicopters-of-wwii.

463. Bothe, "Brief History of Freeman Field—the Fact Sheet."

464. Ibid.

465. Ibid.

466. Larry Bothe, "Freeman Army Airfield Museum: Museum History," Freeman Army Airfield Museum, accessed December 2, 2022, https://freemanarmyairfieldmuseum.org/history-of-the-museum.

467. Dorothy Riker, "Jefferson Proving Ground," in *The Hoosier Training Ground: A History of Army and Navy Training Centers, Camps, Forts, Depots, and Other Military Installations Within the State Boundaries During World War II*, ed. Dorothy Riker (Bloomington: Indiana War History Commission, 1952), 311; Jefferson Proving Ground (JPG) Heritage Partnership, *Reminiscences and Reflections: An Oral History of Dramatic Contrast between Hoosiers and the War Department in Southern Indiana*, eds. Ken Knouf, Mike Moore, Louis Munier and Ron Harsin (N.p.: Trafford Publishing, 2010), 90.

468. Riker, "Jefferson Proving Ground," 317.

469. Ibid., 309.

470. Ibid., 305–6.

471. Ibid., 307.

472. Jefferson Proving Ground (JPG) Heritage Partnership, *Reminiscences and Reflections*, 15.

473. Ibid., 128.

474. Ibid., 129–30.

475. Jefferson Proving Ground (JPG) Heritage Partnership, *Reminiscences and Reflections*, 89; Riker, "Jefferson Proving Ground," 314.

476. Jefferson Proving Ground (JPG) Heritage Partnership, *Reminiscences and Reflections*, xv; Riker, "Jefferson Proving Ground," 314.

477. Riker, "Jefferson Proving Ground," 313.

478. Ibid., 314.

479. Ibid., 309.

480. Jefferson Proving Ground (JPG) Heritage Partnership, *Reminiscences and Reflections*, 120; Bill Ladd, "Open House at Proving Grounds Proves 14,000 Are Curious," *Courier-Journal* (Louisville, KY), November 2, 1941, 1, https://www.newspapers.com/image/108371100/?terms=Jefferson%20Proving%20Ground&match=1.

481. Jefferson Proving Ground (JPG) Heritage Partnership, *Reminiscences and Reflections*, 145–46.

482. Ibid., 111–12; Riker, "Jefferson Proving Ground," 309.

483. Jefferson Proving Ground (JPG) Heritage Partnership, *Reminiscences and Reflections*, 113–14.

484. Ibid., 112.

485. Ibid., 115.
486. Ibid., 102.
487. Riker, "Jefferson Proving Ground," 312.
488. Jefferson Proving Ground (JPG) Heritage Partnership, *Reminiscences and Reflections*, 118.
489. Ibid., 164.
490. Ibid., 319.
491. Ibid., xix.
492. Ibid., 323.
493. Ibid., 319.
494. Ibid., 90.
495. Ibid., xv.
496. National Park Service, "Evansville, Indiana," accessed December 20, 2022, https://www.nps.gov/places/evanston-indiana.htm.
497. "Evansville Accomplished the Extraordinary," banner, Evansville Wartime Museum.
498. Sarah Loesch, "Evansville Wartime Museum to Open for Public," *Evansville (IN) Courier and Press*, May 24, 2017, 1A, https://www.newspapers.com/image/761079455/?terms=Evansville%20Wartime%20Museum.
499. Evansville Wartime Museum, "Experience Homefront Victory!," accessed December 19, 2022, https://www.evansvillewartimemuseum.org.
500. Only 5 percent of the nation's 4,283 top war producing facilities received the award, which was presented for outstanding quality and quantity. Evansville Wartime Museum, information card.
501. Evansville Wartime Museum, information card on Chrysler Motor Plant; Roy Morris Jr., "Evansville, Indiana: World War II's Can-Do-City," HistoryNet, March 23, 2022, https://www.historynet.com/evansville-indiana-world-war-iis-can-do-city.
502. Evansville Wartime Museum, information card on Evansville Shipyard; Morris Jr., "Evansville, Indiana."
503. Evansville Wartime Museum, information card on Republic Aviation; Morris Jr., "Evansville, Indiana."
504. Wikipedia, "Republic Aviation," accessed December 20, 2022, https://en.wikipedia.org/w/index.php?title=Republic_Aviation&oldid=1081455241.
505. May, *Our Service Our Stories*, 3:1–2.
506. Ibid., 5, 7.

507. Ibid., 8.

508. Ibid., 18.

509. Ibid., 19–21.

510. Evansville Wartime Museum, information card on Evansville Red Cross Canteen.

511. Brook Endale, "P-47 Thunderbolt Could Be Official State Aircraft," *Evansville (IN) Courier and Press*, January 14, 2021, A3, https://www.newspapers.com/image/753390148/?terms=Evansville%20Wartime%20Museum&match=1.

512. Aaron Chatman, "Historic WWII Tank Collected by Evansville Wartime Museum," *Eyewitness News* (WEHT/WTVW), May 25, 2022, https://www.tristatehomepage.com/news/local-news/historic-wwii-tank-collected-by-evansville-wartime-museum/?utm_source=weht-wtvw_app&utm_medium=social&utm_content=share-link.

513. Evansville Wartime Museum, information card on LCVP 325 display.

514. "US Government's Office of Production Management stopped manufacturing of all cars, commercial trucks and auto parts in February 1942. Production resumed October 1945." Evansville Wartime Museum, information card.

515. Jill Lyman, "Evansville Designated as American World War II Heritage City," *14News*, accessed December 20, 2022, https://www.14news.com/2022/12/06/evansville-designated-american-world-war-ii-heritage-city/?fbclid=IwAR0xrPKynqGy_fN9bgTfSAYD-uJjBkSn0mDdMeBglhrJHxXbFVsBzWCgYvU.

516. National Park Service, "American World War II Heritage City Program," accessed December 20, 2022, https://www.nps.gov/subjects/worldwarii/americanheritagecity.htm.

517. LST 393, "LST History," accessed December 15, 2022, https://www.lst393.org/history/lst-general.html.

518. NavSource Online, "Amphibious Photo Archive," Tank Landing Ship LST-325, accessed December 15, 2022, http://www.navsource.org/archives/10/16/160325.htm.

519. Wikipedia, "USS LST-325," accessed December 15, 2022, https://en.wikipedia.org/w/index.php?title=USS_LST-325&oldid=1098594434; Wikipedia, "Landing Ship, Tank," accessed December 15, 2022, https://en.wikipedia.org/w/index.php?title=Landing_Ship,_Tank&oldid=1126161646.

520. Wikipedia, "Landing Ship, Tank."

521. Ibid.

522. Although the navy did not expect the ships to last long, more than 1,000 of the 1,051 built survived the war. Half of them were scrapped, 200 were converted for commercial use and the rest were sold to other nations. Despite their slow speed and lack of robust defense, only 26 of the ships were sunk. LST 393, "LST History," accessed December 15, 2022, https://www.lst393.org/history/lst-general.html.

523. Ronald P. May, *Our Service Our Stories* (Martinsville, IN: Fideli Publishing, 2015), 201.

524. Ibid., 202.

525. Ibid., 202–3.

526. Ibid., 203–4.

527. Wikipedia, "Missouri Valley Bridge & Iron Co.," accessed December 16, 2022, https://en.wikipedia.org/w/index.php?title=Missouri_Valley_Bridge_%26_Iron_Co.&oldid=1092726228. Jeffersonville, Indiana, 125 miles upstream from Evansville and on the other side of the river from Louisville, also had a shipyard during World War II. The U.S. Navy bought it and renamed it the Jeffersonville Boat & Machine Company. It built 123 LSTs along with 23 submarines. Wikipedia, "Jeffboat," accessed December 16, 2022, https://en.wikipedia.org/w/index.php?title=Jeffboat&oldid=1077713663.

528. David Bronson, *Mosier's Raiders: The Story of LST-325, 1942–1946* (N.p.: iUniverse Inc., 2004), 1, 15.

529. David Bronson, "The USS LST Ship Memorial History," USS LST-325 | WWII Landing Ship, accessed December 16, 2022, https://www.lstmemorial.org/history.

530. Ibid.

531. Ibid.

532. Ibid.

533. Ibid.

534. Captain Bob Jornlin, CO, "M/V LST Ship Memorial" (pdf), https://www.google.com/url?sa=t&rct=j&q=&esrc=s&source=web&cd=&ved=2ahUKEwiQie6jqf77AhXMEUQIHZ0qDbIQFnoECBMQAQ&url=https%3A%2F%2Firp.cdn-website.com%2F899cd00d%2Ffiles%2Fuploaded%2FCaptain%252BJornlin%252BPersonal%252BAccount.pdf&usg=AOvVaw2uNX9GrnlOEzMxQ8Lxc7Ng.

535. Ibid.

536. Ibid.

537. Ibid.

538. Ibid.

539. Wikipedia, "USS LST-325."

540. Visit https://www.lst393.org for more information on LST 393.

541. This chapter is a revision of two articles the author wrote in 2018 for the *Martinsville (IN) Reporter-Times*. Ronald P. May, "Built for War: The Story of a World War II Amphibious Ship," *Martinsville (IN) Reporter-Times*, May 12, 2018, 1 and 7; Ronald P. May, "LST 32 Finds a Home in the 'Cornfield Shipyards,'" *Martinsville (IN) Reporter-Times*, May 18, 2018, 1 and 6.

542. Glenn Spencer, *The Boys of Boomtown* (N.p.: printed by the author, 2015), 3.

543. Rob Vest, "Charlestown, IN, and the Indiana Army Ammunition Plant: The Making of a War-Industry Boom-Town," Indiana University Southeast, https://web.archive.org/web/20060906204049/http://homepages.ius.edu/RVEST/INAAP.htm.

544. Nicole Poletika, "World War II Comes to Indiana: The Indiana Army Ammunition Plant, Part I," Indiana History Blog, February 23, 2016, https://blog.history.in.gov/world-war-ii-comes-to-indiana-the-indiana-army-ammunition-plant-part-i.

545. Charlestown-Clark County: Genealogy—Indiana Army Ammunition Plant, "The Library's Collection of Artifacts and Brief History of Indiana Ordnance Works, Indiana Arsenal, Hoosier Ordnance Plant, and Indiana Army Ammunition Plant," accessed December 20, 2022, http://clarkco.lib.in.us/contentpages.asp?loc=118; Vest, "Charlestown, IN, and the Indiana Army Ammunition Plant."

546. Abandoned, "Indiana Army Ammunition Plant," March 4, 2022, https://abandonedonline.net/location/indiana-army-ammunition-plant.

547. Ibid.

548. Abandoned, "Indiana Army Ammunition Plant."

549. Vest, "Charlestown, IN, and the Indiana Army Ammunition Plant."

550. Charlestown-Clark County: Genealogy—Indiana Army Ammunition Plant, "Library's Collection of Artifacts"; Vest, "Charlestown, IN, and the Indiana Army Ammunition Plant."

551. Abandoned, "Indiana Army Ammunition Plant."

552. Charlestown-Clark County: Genealogy—Indiana Army Ammunition Plant, "Library's Collection of Artifacts"; Vest, "Charlestown, IN, and the Indiana Army Ammunition Plant."

553. Charlestown-Clark County: Genealogy—Indiana Army Ammunition Plant, "Library's Collection of Artifacts"; Vest, "Charlestown, IN, and the Indiana Army Ammunition Plant."

554. Abandoned, "Indiana Army Ammunition Plant."

555. Charlestown-Clark County: Genealogy—Indiana Army Ammunition Plant, "Library's Collection of Artifacts."

556. Ibid.

557. Nicole Poletika, "World War II Comes to Indiana: The Indiana Army Ammunition Plant, Part II," Indiana History Blog, February 25, 2016, https://blog.history.in.gov/world-war-ii-comes-to-indiana-the-indiana-army-ammunition-plant-part-ii; Vest, "Charlestown, IN, and the Indiana Army Ammunition Plant."

558. Vest, "Charlestown, IN, and the Indiana Army Ammunition Plant."

559. Charlestown-Clark County: Genealogy—Indiana Army Ammunition Plant, "Library's Collection of Artifacts."

560. Robert Kelly, *Broken Wings* (N.p.: Conn Publishing, 2009), 38–39.

561. Robert Kelly, in a phone conversation with the author, November 15, 2022.

562. Ibid., 100.

563. Abandoned, "Indiana Army Ammunition Plant."

564. Vest, "Charlestown, IN, and the Indiana Army Ammunition Plant."

565. Charlestown-Clark County: Genealogy—Indiana Army Ammunition Plant, "Library's Collection of Artifacts."

566. Poletika, "World War II Comes to Indiana, Part II."

567. Vest, "Charlestown, IN, and the Indiana Army Ammunition Plant."

568. Charlestown-Clark County: Genealogy—Indiana Army Ammunition Plant, "Library's Collection of Artifacts."

569. Indiana Historical Bureau, "WWII Army Ammunition Plant," December 9, 2022, https://www.in.gov/history/state-historical-markers/find-a-marker/find-historical-markers-by-county/indiana-historical-markers-by-county/wwii-army-ammunition-plant.

BIBLIOGRAPHY

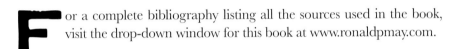or a complete bibliography listing all the sources used in the book, visit the drop-down window for this book at www.ronaldpmay.com.

ABOUT THE AUTHOR

Ron May has served as a chaplain, pastor and freelance writer. He spent twenty-five years in full-time church ministry as a Lutheran pastor. For twenty-two of those years, he also served in the armed forces as a navy reserve chaplain. In 2012, following his retirement from the navy, Ron began work as a freelance writer, submitting the stories of military veterans for publication in local newspapers. He is the author of a multivolume book series, *Our Service Our Stories*, which features the service stories of Indiana World War II veterans. In December 2020, Ron completed his master's degree in World War II studies from Arizona State University. Ron serves as chaplain at Hoosier Village Retirement Community in Zionsville and resides in Carmel, Indiana, with his wife, Glenda. You can contact him at ron@ronaldpmay.com. Visit his website at www.ronaldpmay.com. You can also visit his YouTube channel at "World War II History and Stories with Ron May." Follow him on Facebook at "Our Service, Our Stories."